Amazing Agent Jennifer

AGENT ASSESSMENT FORM

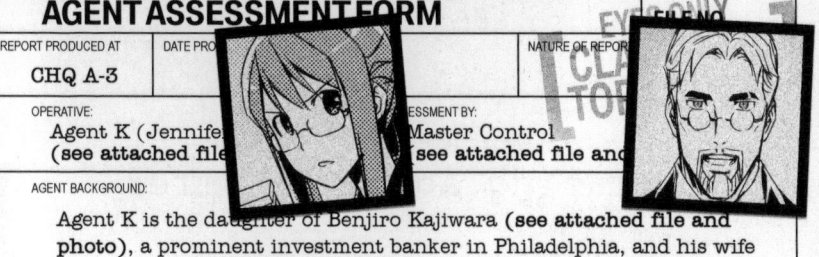

REPORT PRODUCED AT	DATE PRO...		NATURE OF REPOR...

CHQ A-3

OPERATIVE:
Agent K (Jennife... ...ESSMENT BY: Master Control
(see attached file... (see attached file and...

AGENT BACKGROUND:

Agent K is the daughter of Benjiro Kajiwara (**see attached file and photo**), a prominent investment banker in Philadelphia, and his wife Emily Kajiwara, née Emily Warren (**see attached file and photo**), from the prominent Warren family of Philadelphia. Agent K exhibited numerous skills in childhood and adolescence. Her most noteworthy pre-Agency accomplishment, however, was in the field of science, where her senior year science project in high school revolutionized the field of genetics and was sent to be studied at the National Institute of Health.

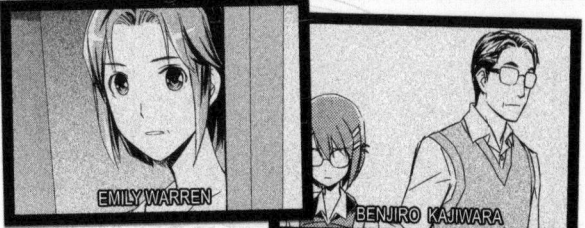

EMILY WARREN

BENJIRO KAJIWARA

ASSESSMENT:

This Control Agent recruited Agent K personally, and believes she is the ideal operative. She excelled at her four-year training course, while maintaining a 4.0 GPA in college, earning valedictorian honors. And she did all this despite having to suffer a breakdown in her relationship with her parents, who wished to control her education and career options.

CURRENT MISSION

Operation Code Retrieval. Agent K is to be sent into Bruckenstein as part of a team tasked with retrieving stolen genetics research—the same research from Agent K's high school science project. She has infiltrated the lab as a janitor, while Agent D (**see attached file and photo**) romances Heinrich Von Brucken (**see attached file and photo**), second son of the nation's ruler. Backup is to be provided by Agent L (**see atta...**

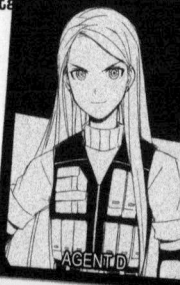

AGENT D

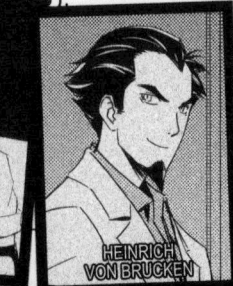

HEINRICH VON BRUCKEN

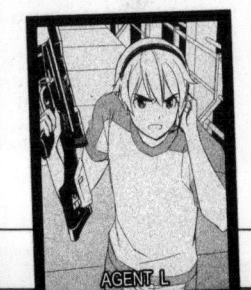

AGENT L

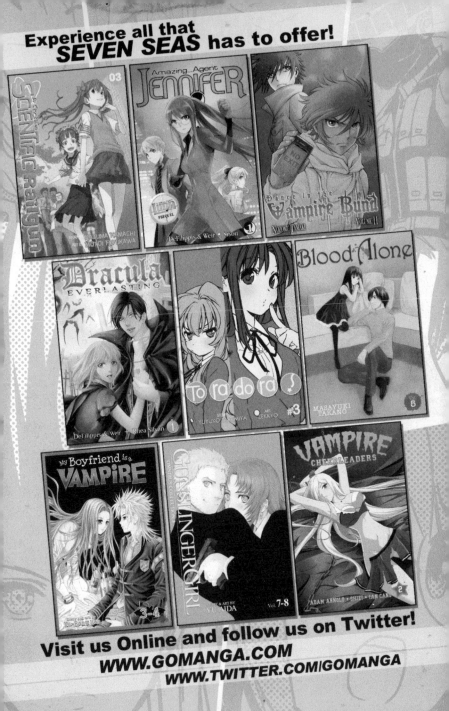

Amazing_Agent
LUNA

From the writers of Amazing_Agent JENNIFER

Experience All 7 Exciting Volumes!

Luna: the perfect secret agent. A girl grown in a lab from the finest genetic material, she has been trained since birth to be the U.S. government's ultimate espionage weapon. But now she is given an assignment that will test her abilities to the max - high school!

story
Nunzio DeFilippis & Christina Weir • *art* Shiei

MEMORANDUM

TO: OUR READERS
FROM: NUNZIO DEFILIPPIS AND CHRISTINA WEIR
RE: AMAZING AGENT JENNIFER VOLUME 2

So, that's it. The story of how Jennifer Kajiwara became Control. Also, the story of how Heinrich Von Brucken became ruler of his tiny country, and how Elyse Douglas became his Countess. And finally, the story of how Project Luna came into existence.

Pulling this story together was tricky. We were inventing something new, filling out corners of the "Lunaverse" into which we'd never truly looked. Yet so many small pieces were already there.

In *Amazing Agent Luna Volume 2*, both Control and her parents recounted how she became so estranged from them. Even within that story, different versions were mentioned by the various players—a choice we made at the time to make it feel like a real fight in a real family. We all remember it differently, and sometimes one person remembers it differently from the last time they talked about it.

In *Luna Volume 3*, a mysterious agent of Bruckenstein broke into the secret base where Luna was being raised and trained. This agent knew something was going on at that lab, and Control recognized her. In *Luna Volume 5*, we clarified that this mysterious agent survived that encounter and that she was Heinrich's wife (and Jonah's mother). That left it so that Control's recognition was simply someone realizing that the spy they're fighting is actually the Countess of a foreign nation.

In *Amazing Agent Luna Volume 5*, we also revealed that Luna was actually Control's daughter, but never really explained how this happened.

So when it came time to write this story, we had a LOT of mixing and matching to do. We wanted to weave a story that was not only Control's origin story, but backstory for the Von Brucken family, and the origin of Luna herself. And, of course, we wanted to tell a story that worked, on its own, as a story of a young woman becoming a kick-ass secret agent.

So where does it go from here? Back to *Amazing Agent Luna*.

Our pasts always influence our future and there were too many rich, juicy details added here that we're not ready to let go of yet. So expect to see elements that were developed in *Amazing Agent Jennifer* explored in future volumes of *Amazing Agent Luna*.

One part of the story that won't appear in *Amazing Agent Luna* is Kriss Sison. Luna is Shiei's book, and that will always be true. But we couldn't be more grateful to Kriss for his role in expanding the Luna-verse and helping us weave this tale. He truly captured the world and brought Jennifer's past to life in a most vibrant and exciting way.

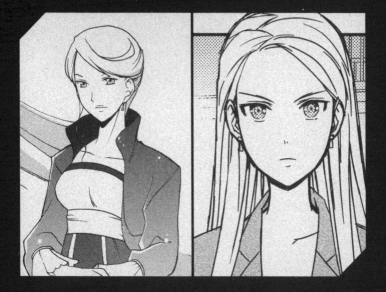

Elyse Douglas married Heinrich Von Brucken to become the Countess of Bruckenstein. Thus, she regained the status and wealth she had lost when her Senator father's career ended in scandal. She and Heinrich had one son, a boy named Jonah. However, Elyse remained an elite level field operative, becoming Bruckenstein's top agent.

She eventually clashed with Jennifer again, and lost that fight, nearly dying in the process. She remained a prisoner of the Agency for 10 years, before her son Jonah rescued her. The two then allowed Heinrich to be arrested for his schemes against the U.S.

Elyse took control of Bruckenstein, using her son as her puppet, but when she tried to destroy all of Manhattan with a fusion device, her son helped the Agency foil the scheme, and allowed her to be arrested as well.

She awaits trial for her many crimes...

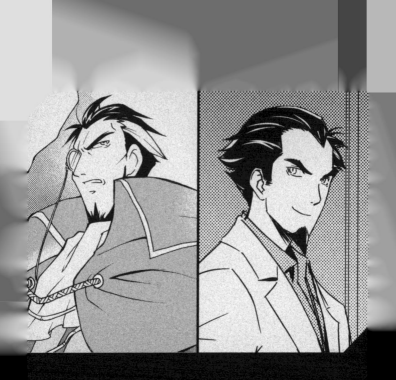

Heinrich Von Brucken remained Count of Bruckenstein until very recently. His anti-U.S. stance grew more vocal, and this led his tiny nation to be further isolated and eventually deemed a "rogue nation." It is a little known fact that Bruckenstein was included on a recent President's list of nations described as an "Axis Of Evil." However since the country was so small, all the major papers removed Bruckenstein from the Axis for space reasons. This only served to infuriate Heinrich more.

He remained obsessed with genetics and tried to steal back the research the country had lost, and eventually concocted schemes of his own involving cloning technology.

Heinrich remained married to Elyse, and they had one son, Jonah. Elyse was eventually captured by the U.S., and Jonah eventually double-crossed Heinrich, who was arrested for anti-U.S. schemes and extradited by his own son.

When Elyse returned to Bruckenstein without him, Heinrich offered to help the U.S. shut down whatever his wife and son were planning.

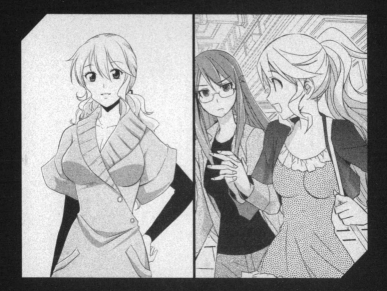

Kimberly Donovan is now the head of the Donovan Modeling Agency.

She briefly married Pierre, but that marriage lasted all of a month. Kim has been in and out of relationships ever since, but none lasted more than a few weeks.

Kim never heard from Jennifer again, and to this day does not know exactly why their friendship resumed and then ended so abruptly.

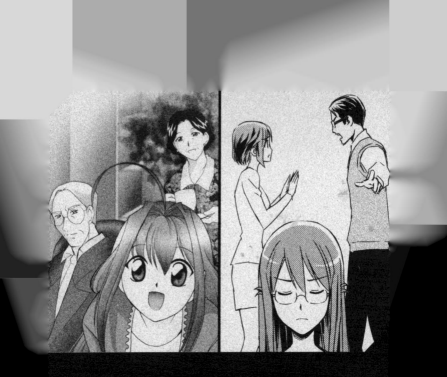

Benjiro and Emily Kajiwara still live in Philadelphia. They did not speak with their daughter for over a decade and a half.

When Luna's principal at Nobel High took it upon herself to make Family Week special for Luna, she contacted Jennifer's parents assuming Luna would enjoy having her grandparents at the school. This was the first contact for Benjiro and Emily with their daughter and their first clue that Jennifer had a "daughter."

The reunion did not go well.

However, the Kajiwaras ended Family Week on speaking terms, so it was still a success.

The Kajiwaras have promised to visit Luna again in the near future.

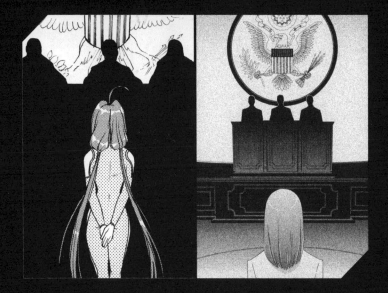

The Agency remains the most secretive of espionage agencies in the United States. Most do not even know it exists, and that includes people in the government.

The faces of the directors of the Agency have never been seen. Jennifer suspects that the same three men who ran the Agency when she was recruited still run it today.

But of that, as well as anything else about the Agency, she cannot be sure.

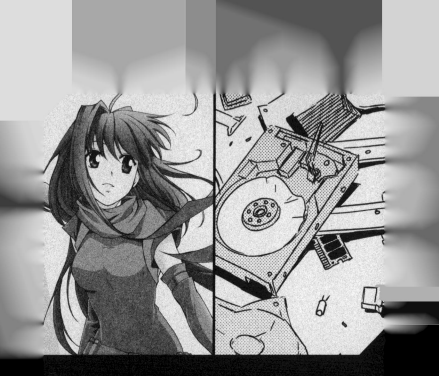

Agent Luna is the result of the work that began with Jennifer Kajiwara's senior year high school science project, and was developed by the United States' National Institute of Health and the scientists of Bruckenstein before finally being perfected by Kajiwara herself at the Agency.

Luna is now 16 years old. Chasing down the plans of the Agency's enemies has led her to go undercover at Nobel High, a private high school for the children of diplomats at the United Nations as well as dignitaries, scientists, and other elites.

Luna was trained by Jennifer to be the perfect secret agent, but not as much on how to deal with her emotions. As a result, Project Luna now has a therapist on staff in the form of Dr. Andrew Collins. Dr. Andy and Jennifer pose as Luna's parents as part of this new assignment, and Luna has come to view them as such.

Luna does not know that Jennifer, who she only knows as "Control,"

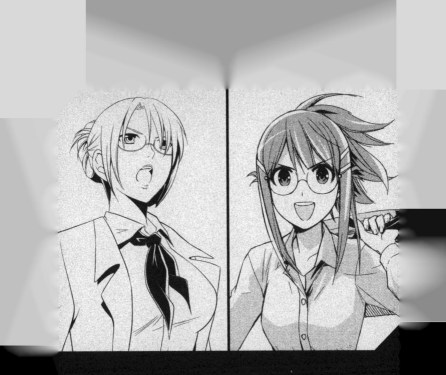

Jennifer Kajiwara has remained with the Agency, and is considered one of their best operatives. As promised, she was given the genetic engineering project and soon "gave birth" to Project Luna. Jennifer was assigned to be Luna's Control agent and began the difficult task of raising a spy.

After the betrayal and loss of Dan Lincoln, Jennifer never again engaged in any romantic relationship until recently. She has finally admitted her feelings for her co-worker on Project Luna, Dr. Andrew Collins.

When making the perfect secret agent, she used her own genetic material for the mother's side of the DNA. The child that was born, Luna, is the culmination of Jennifer's life's work. Jennifer remains the now-teenaged agent's Control Agent, and is known to most

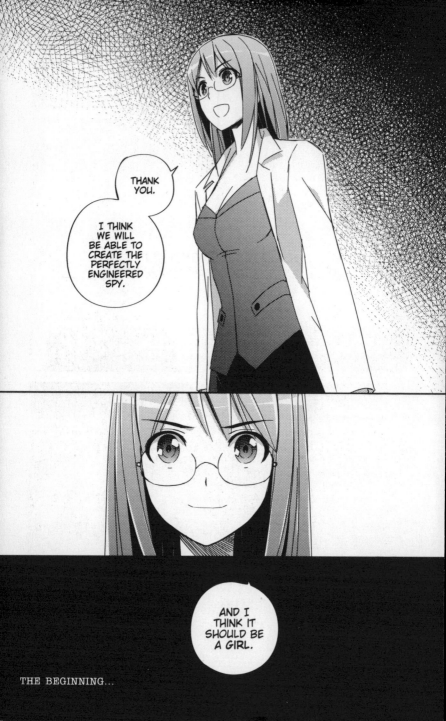

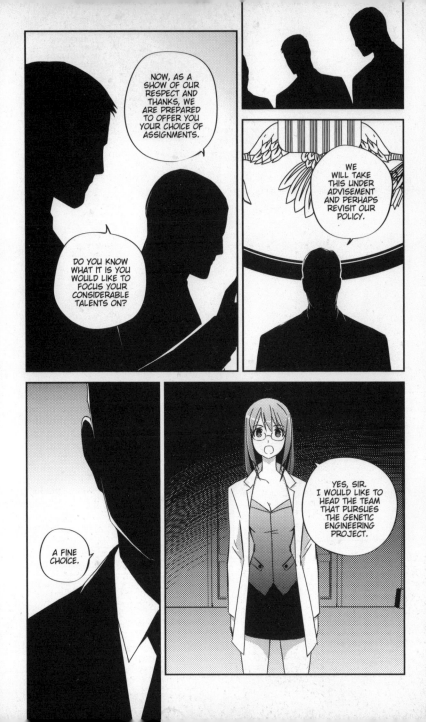

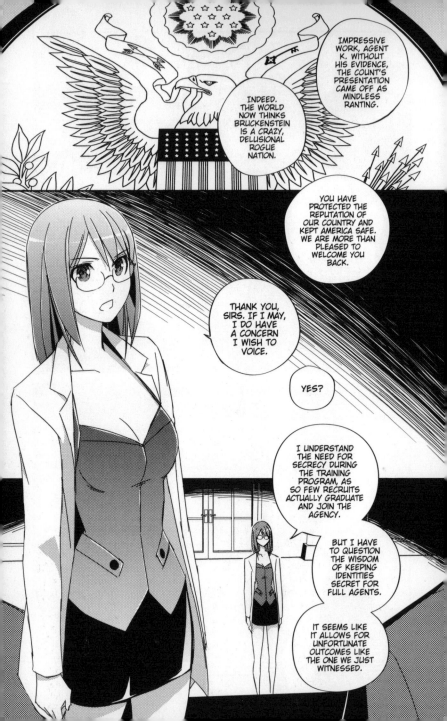

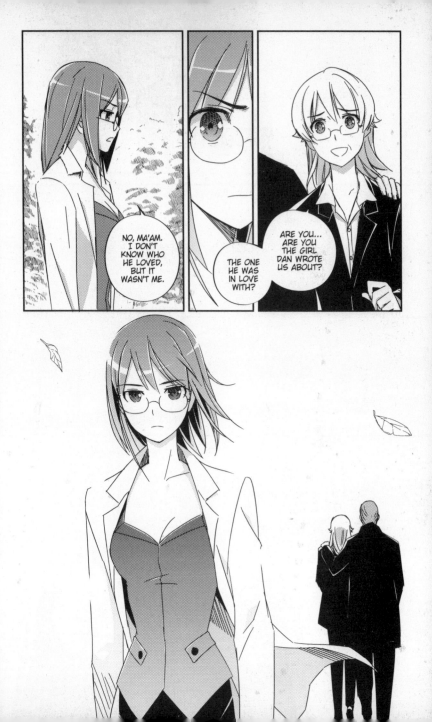

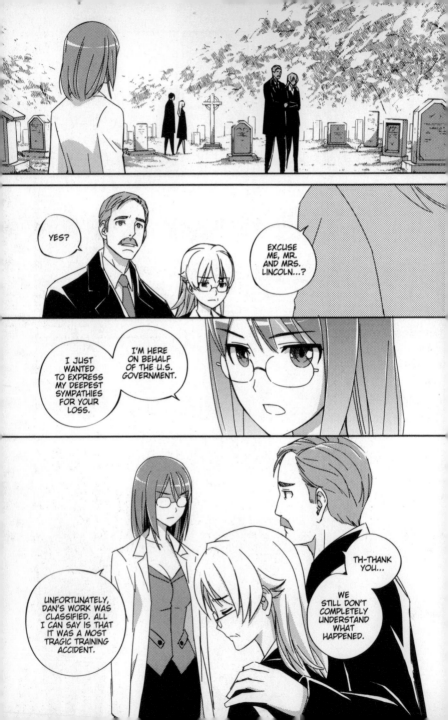

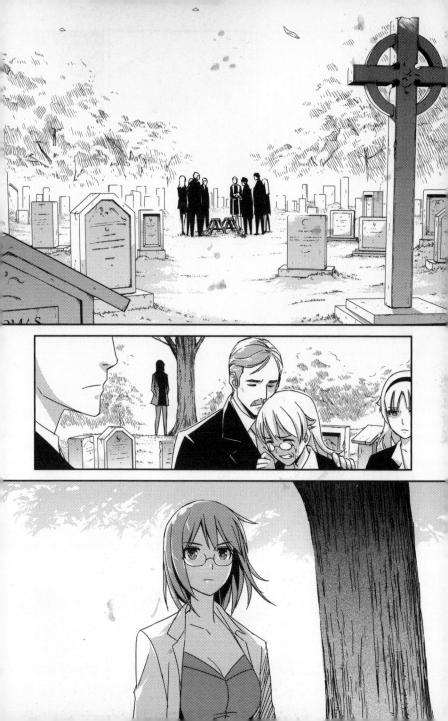

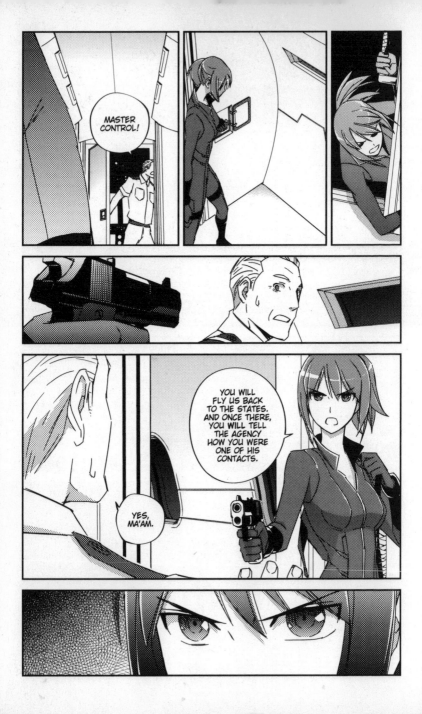

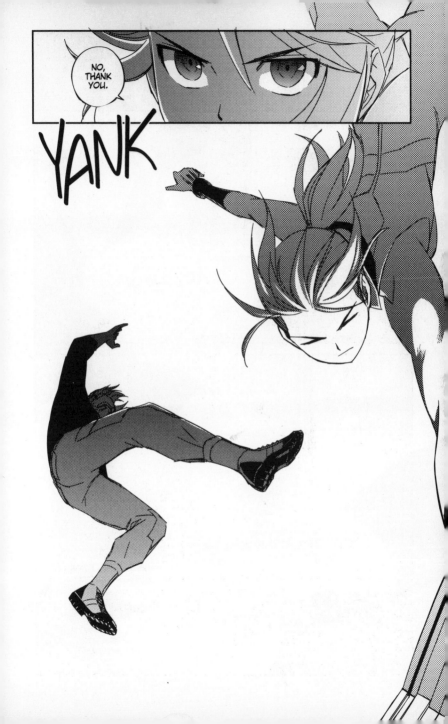

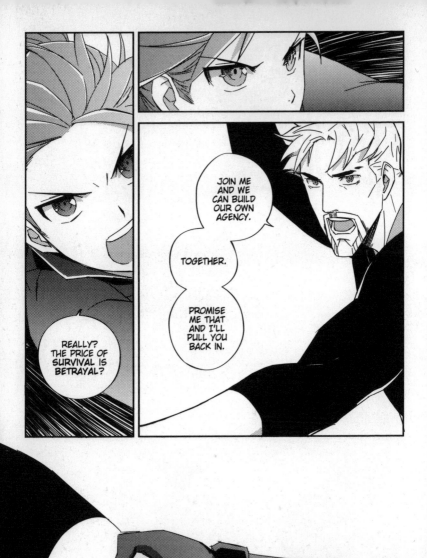

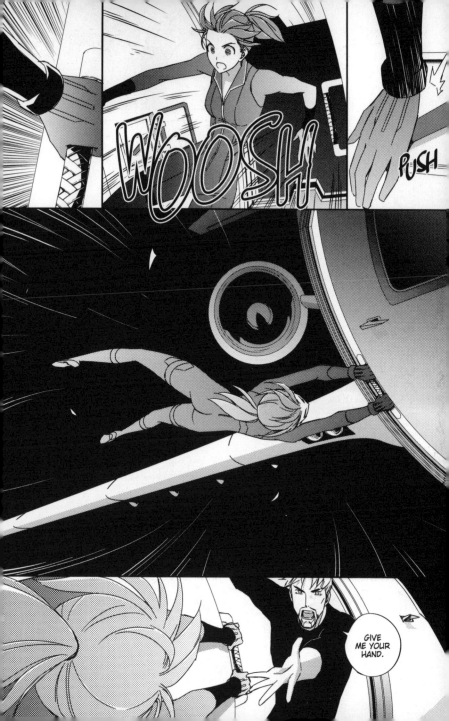

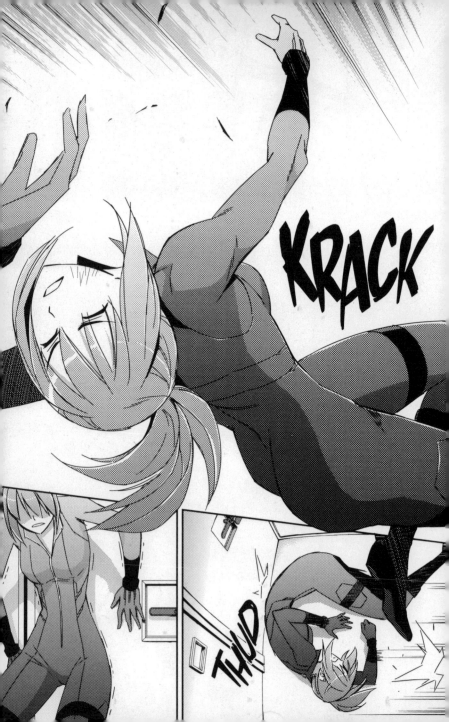

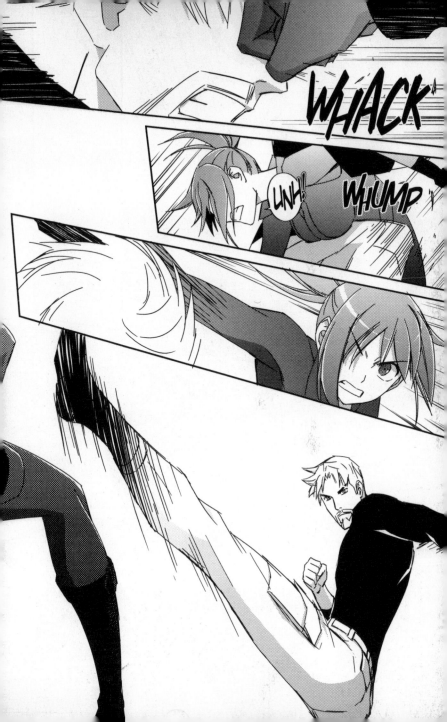

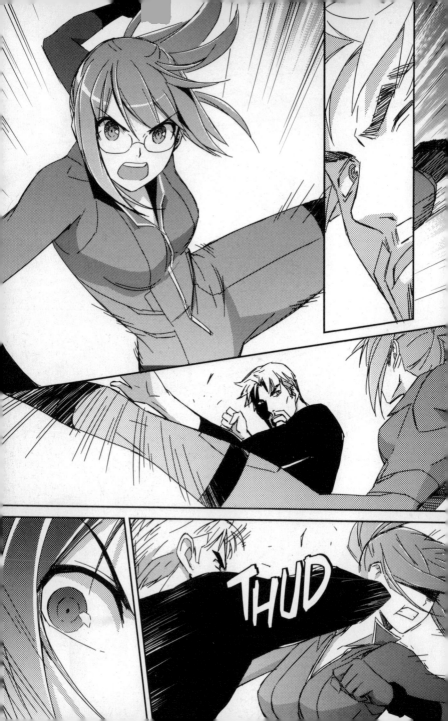

THUD

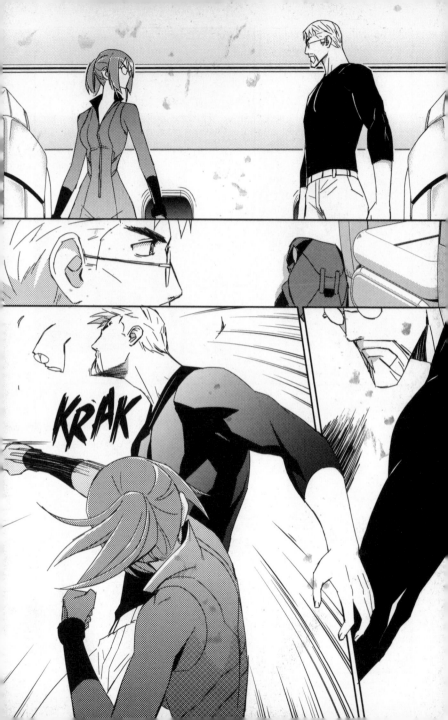

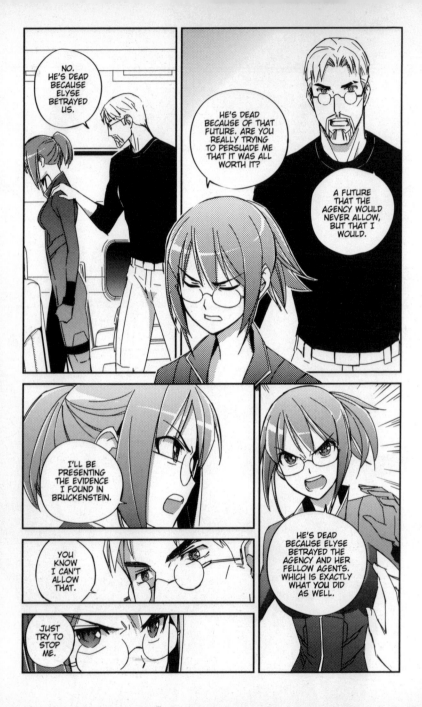

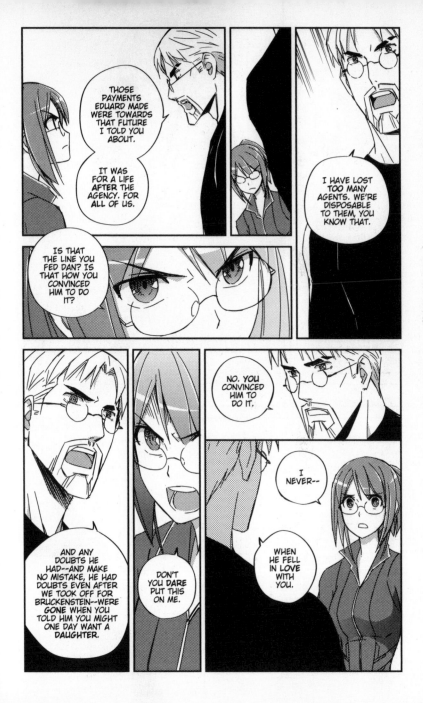

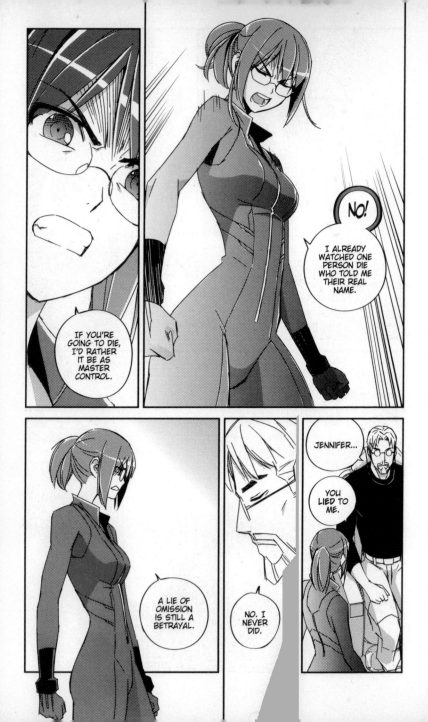

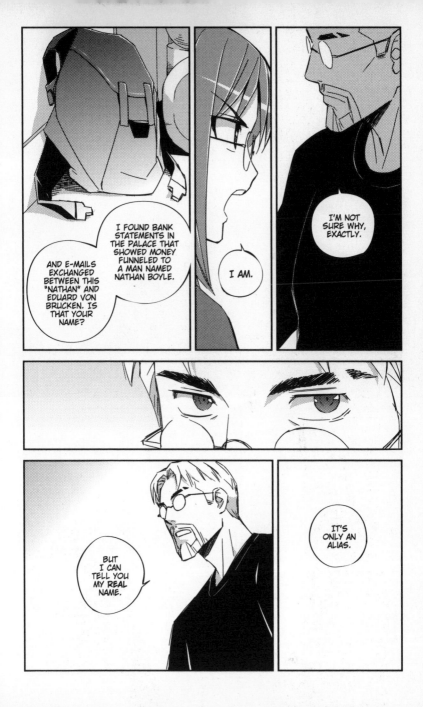

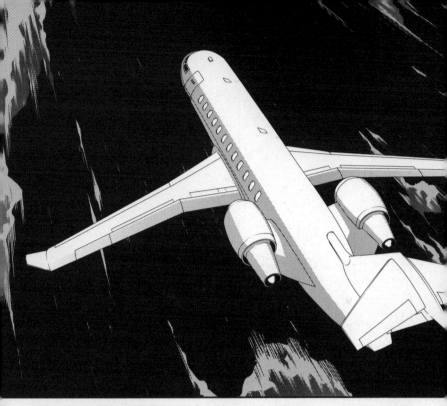

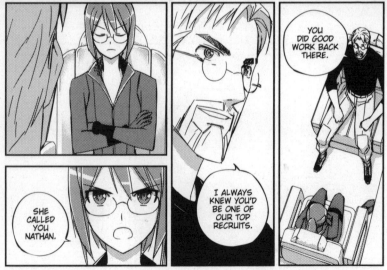

YOU DID *GOOD* WORK BACK THERE.

I ALWAYS KNEW YOU'D BE ONE OF OUR TOP RECRUITS.

SHE CALLED YOU NATHAN.

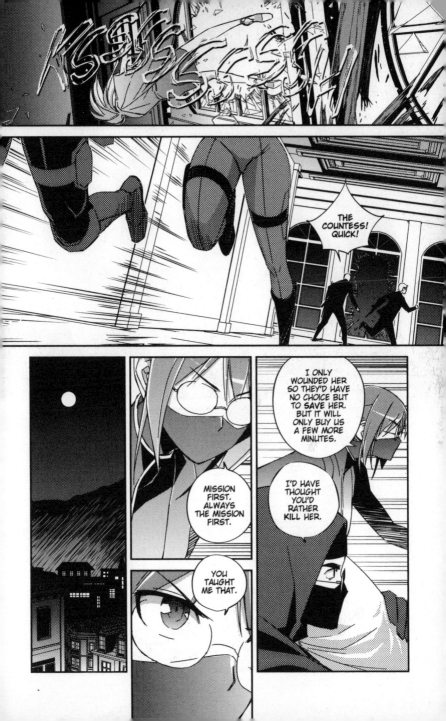

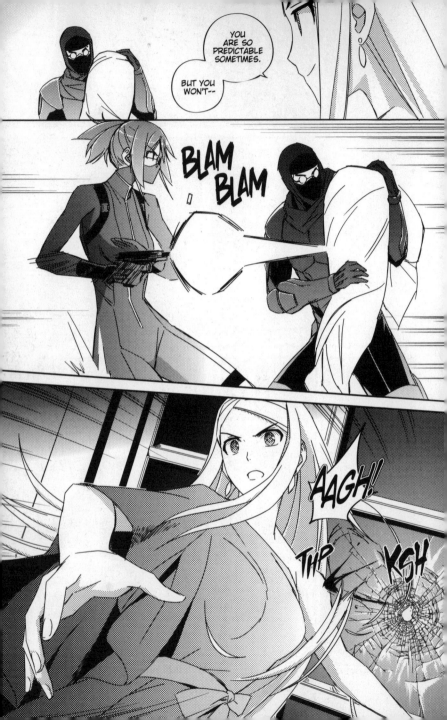

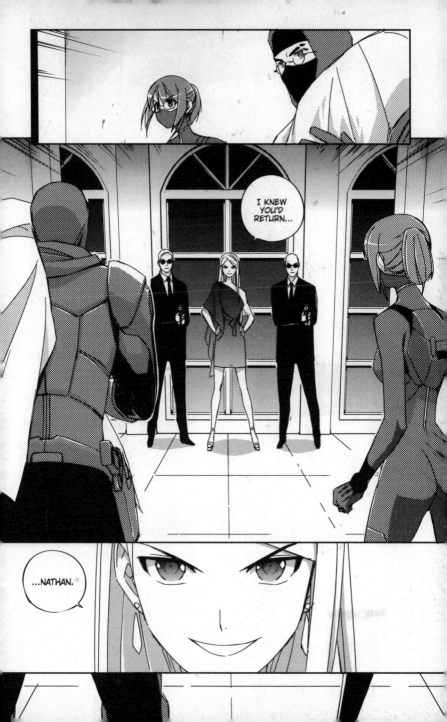

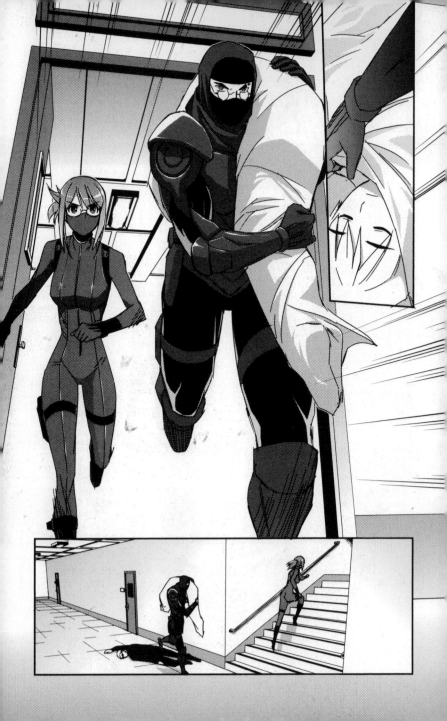

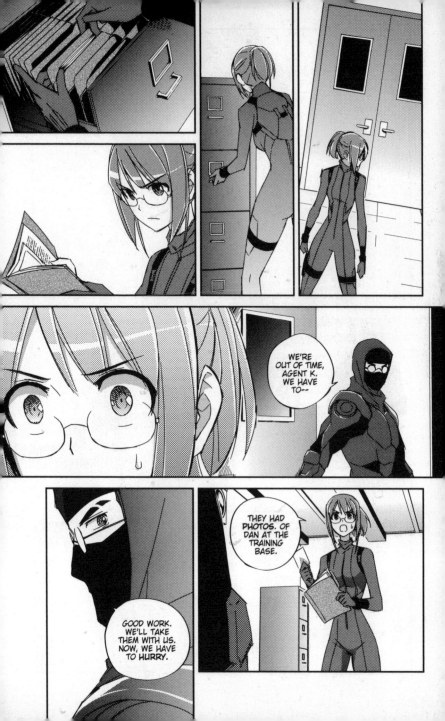

WE'RE OUT OF TIME, AGENT K. WE HAVE TO--

THEY HAD PHOTOS. OF DAN AT THE TRAINING BASE.

GOOD WORK. WE'LL TAKE THEM WITH US. NOW, WE HAVE TO HURRY.

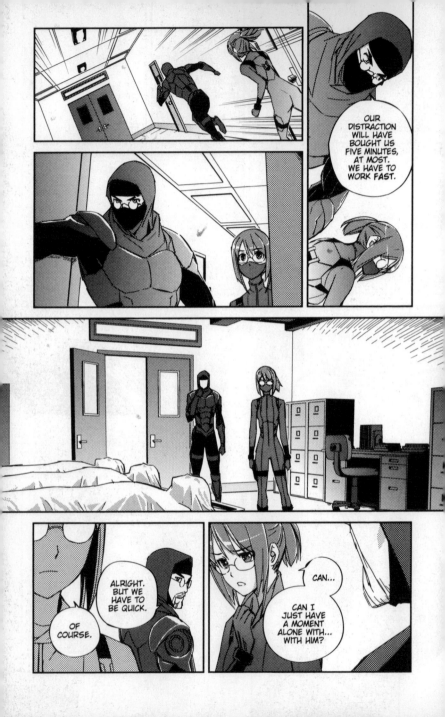

OUR DISTRACTION WILL HAVE BOUGHT US FIVE MINUTES, AT MOST. WE HAVE TO WORK FAST.

ALRIGHT. BUT WE HAVE TO BE QUICK.

OF COURSE.

CAN...

CAN I JUST HAVE A MOMENT ALONE WITH... WITH HIM?

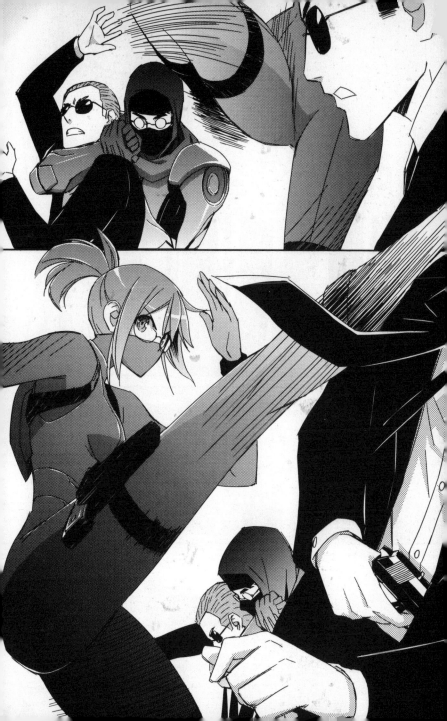

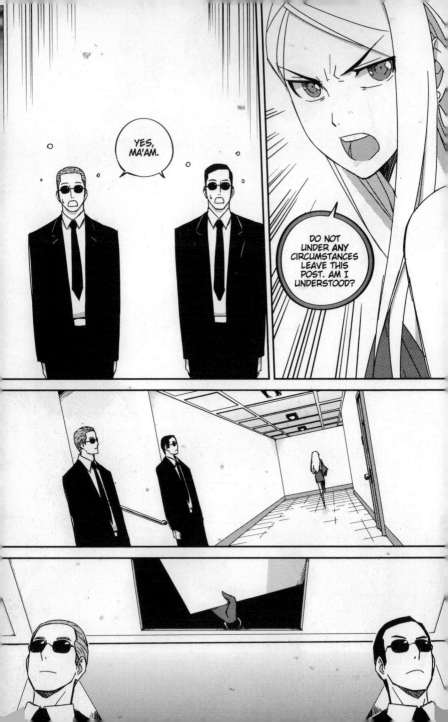

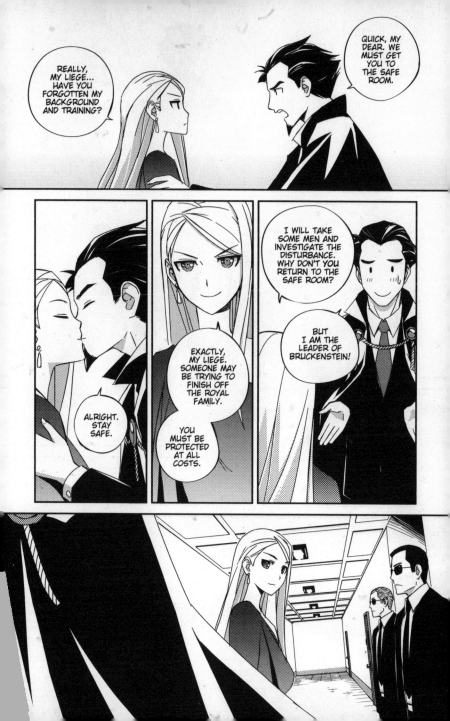

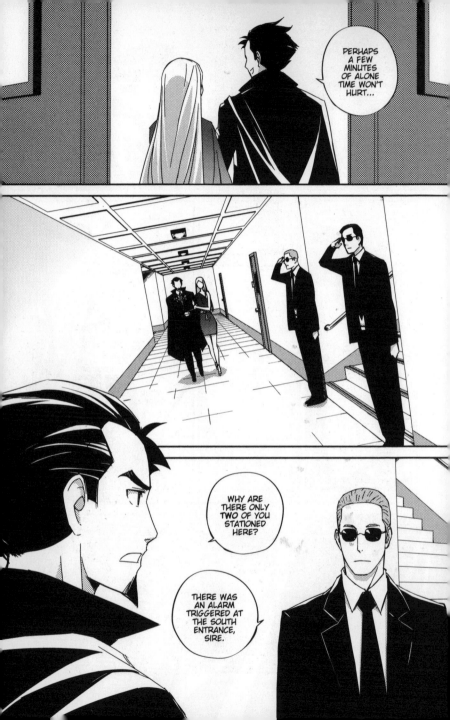

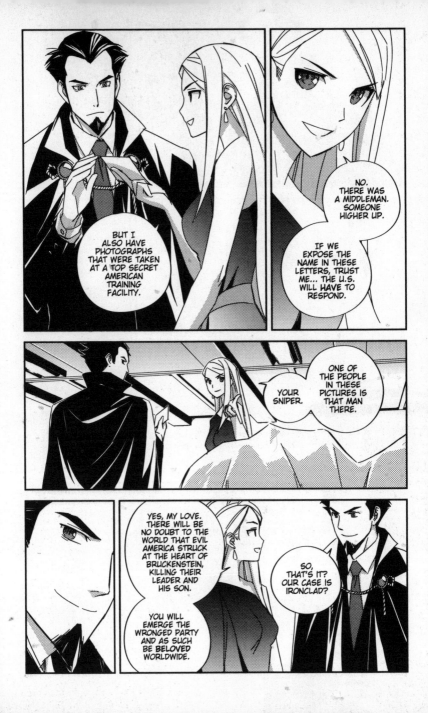

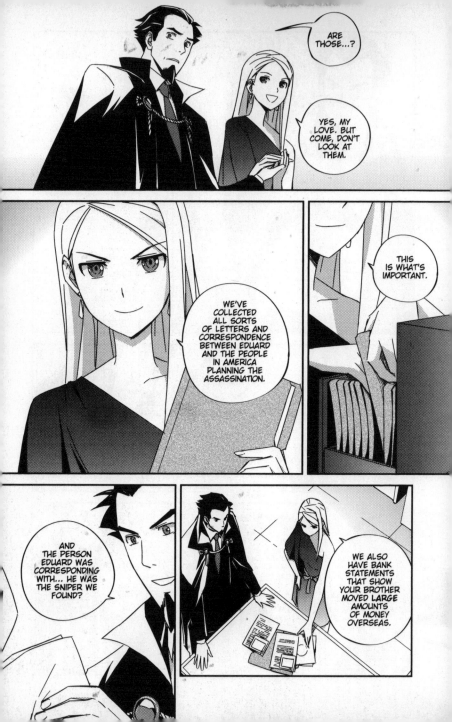

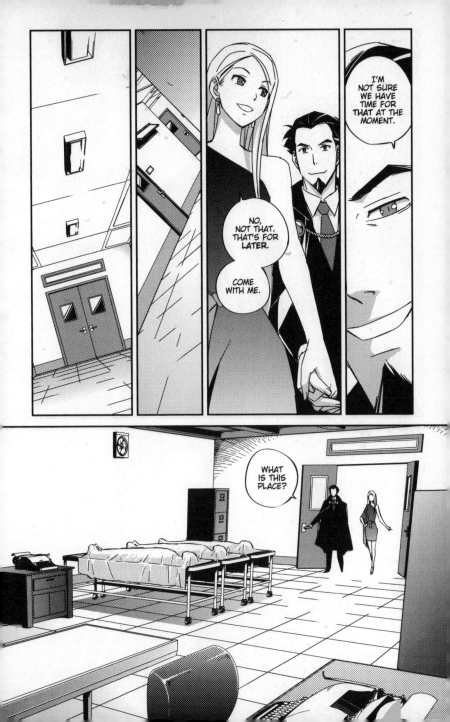

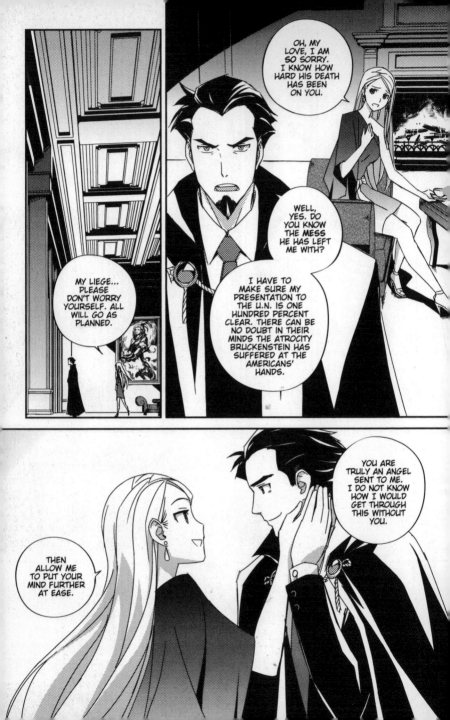

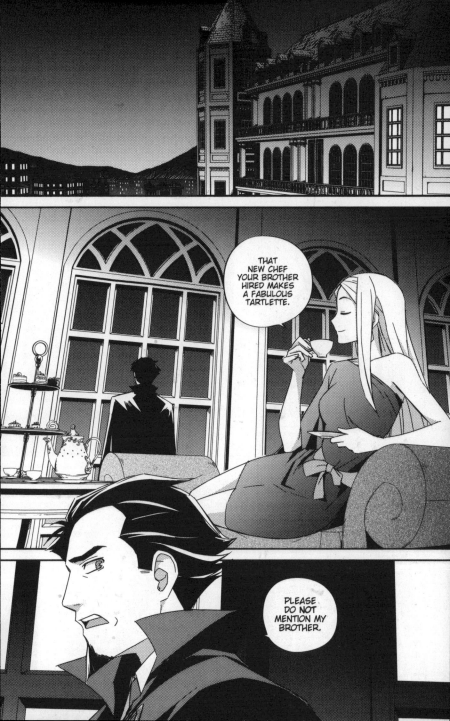

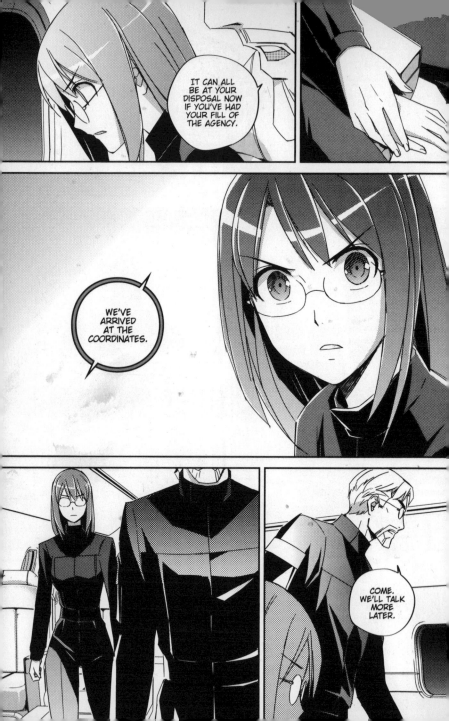

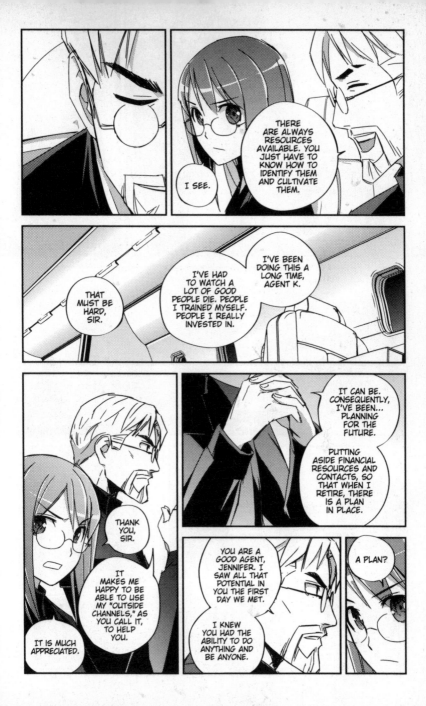

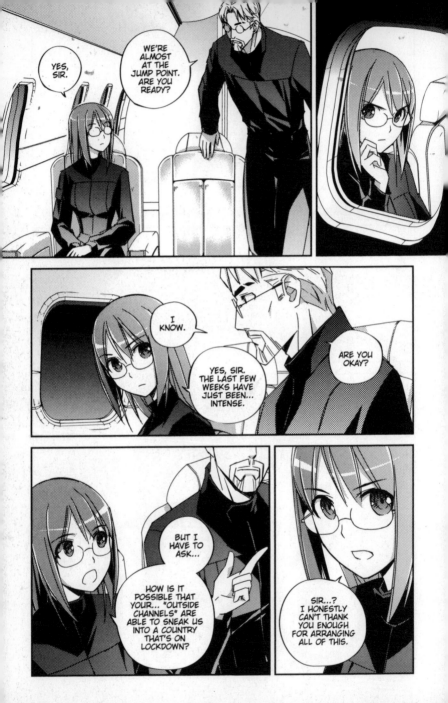

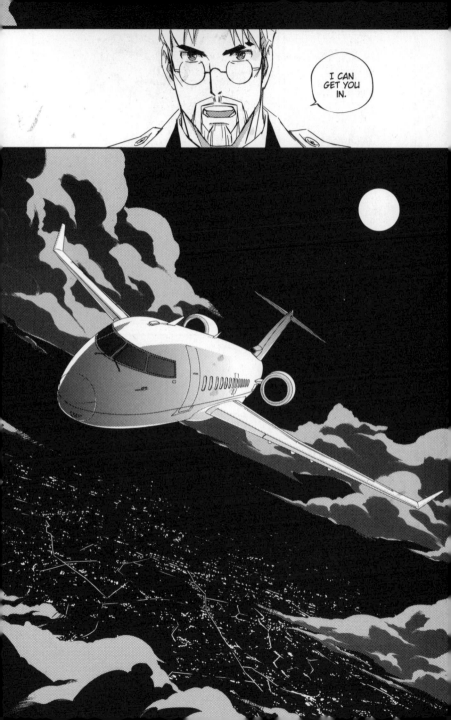

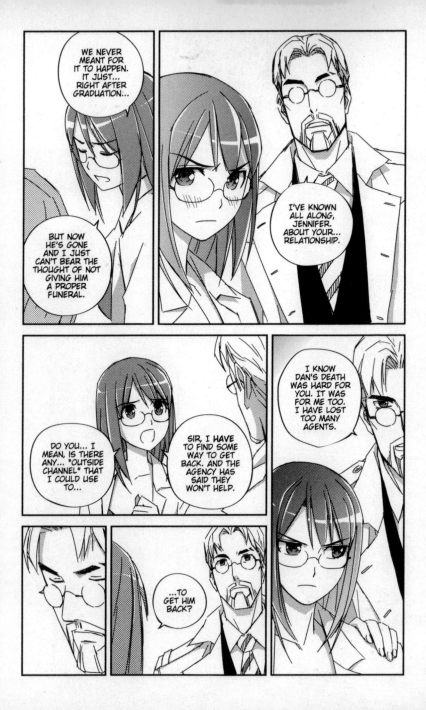

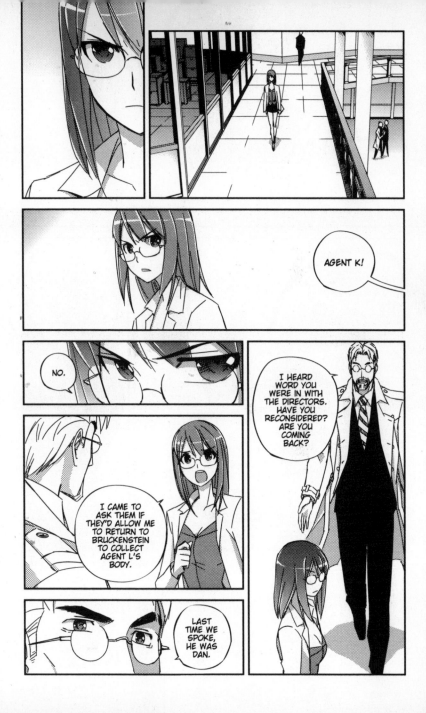

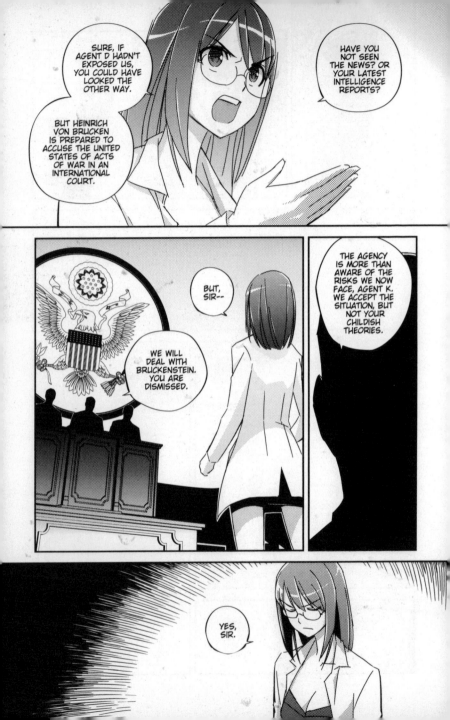

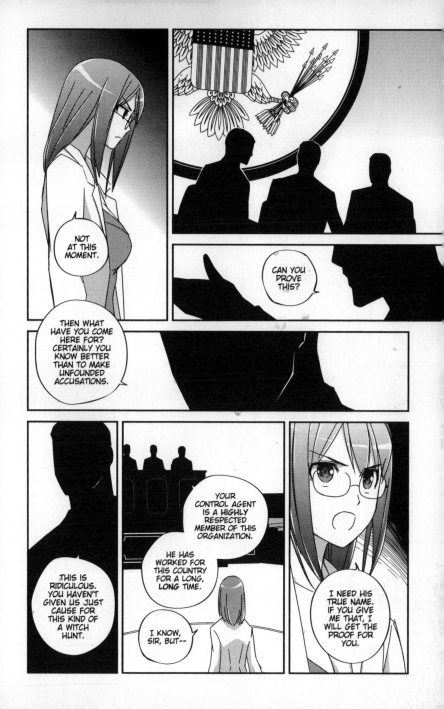

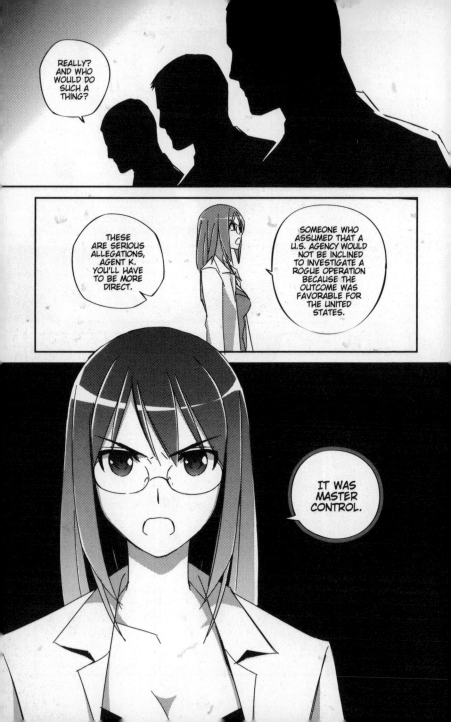

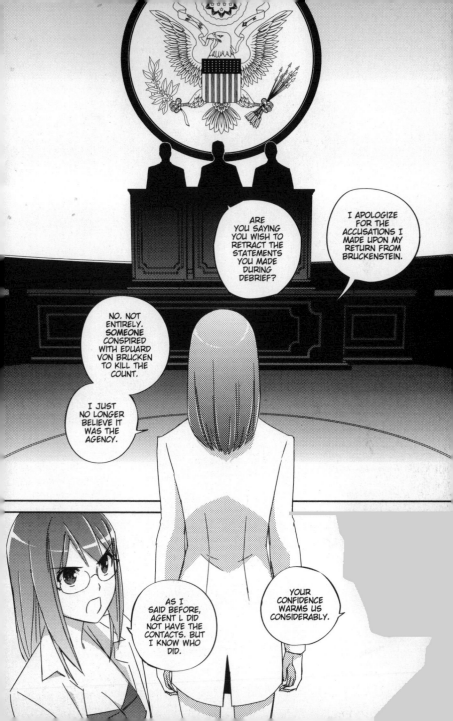

FILE 10:
ENDINGS AND BEGINNINGS

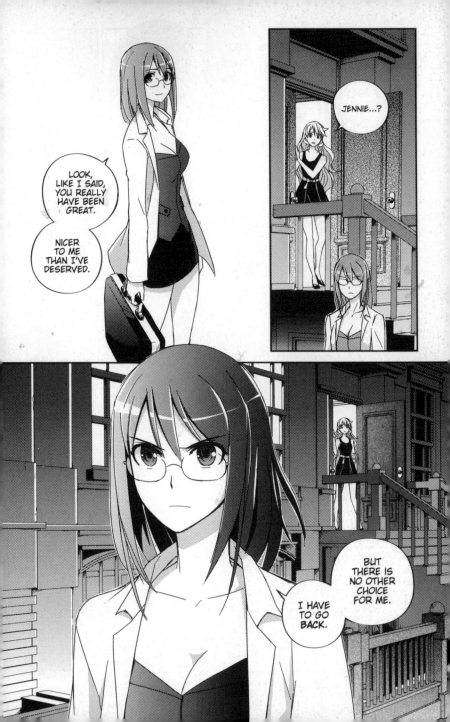

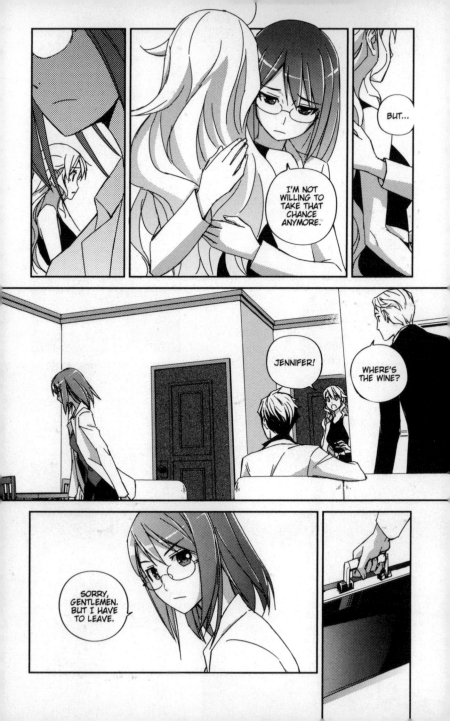

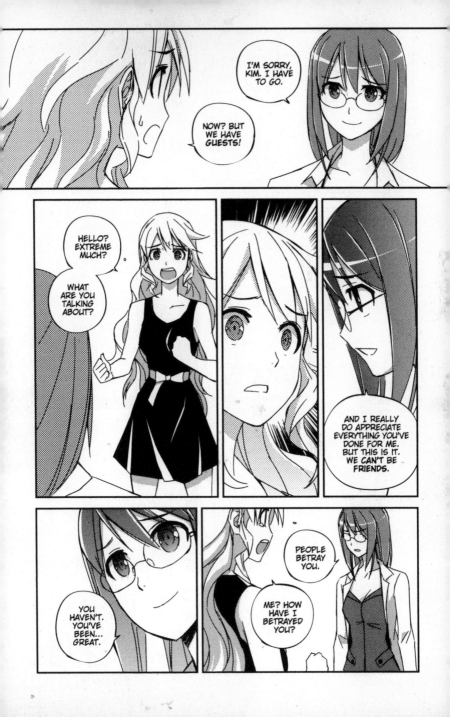

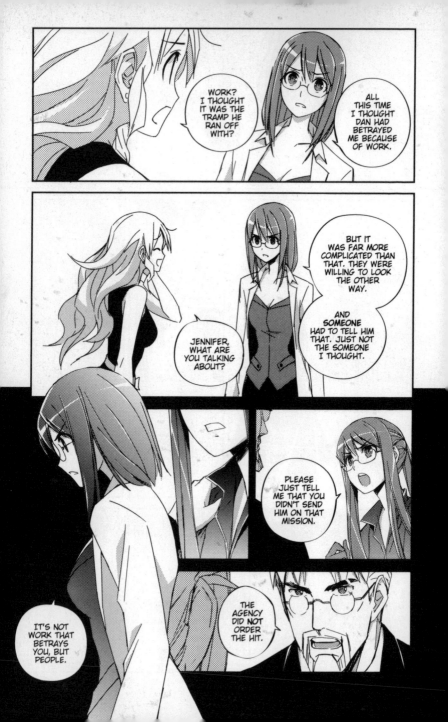

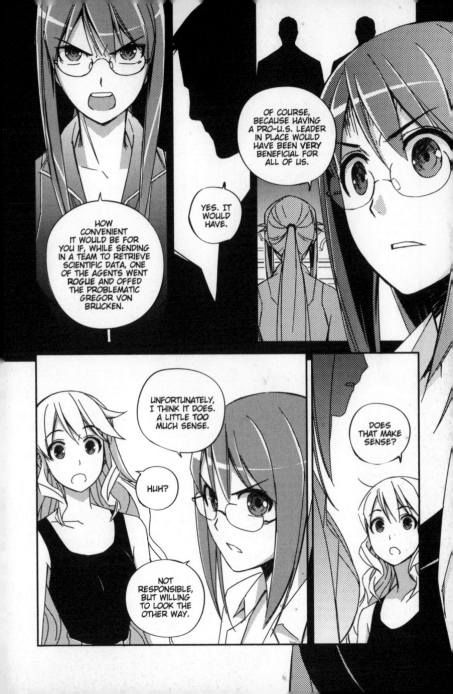

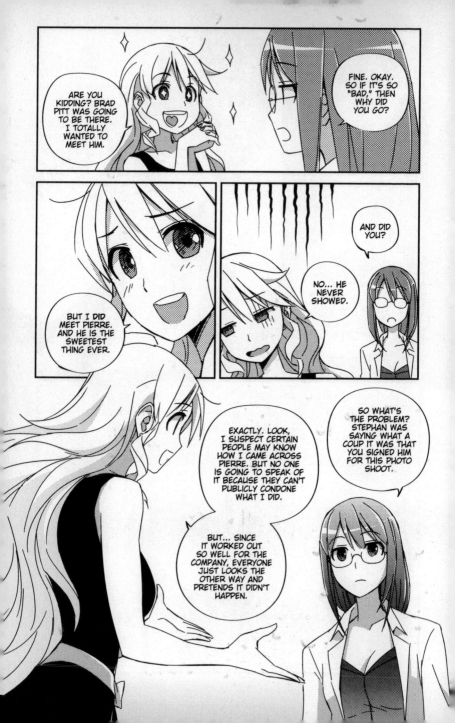

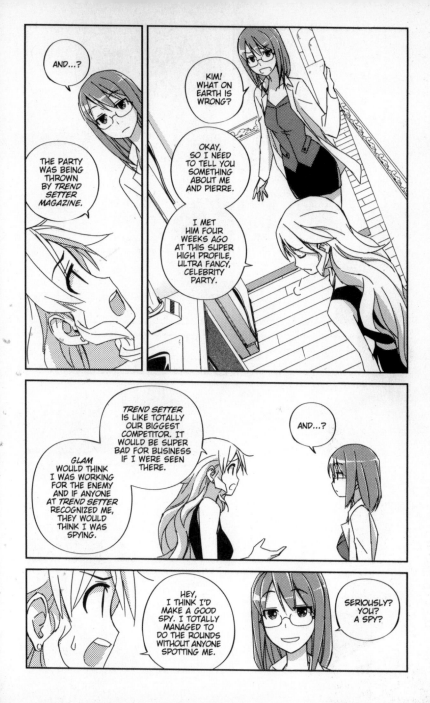

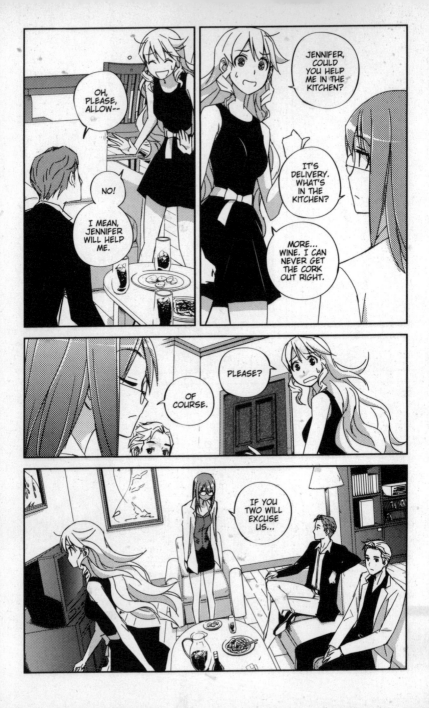

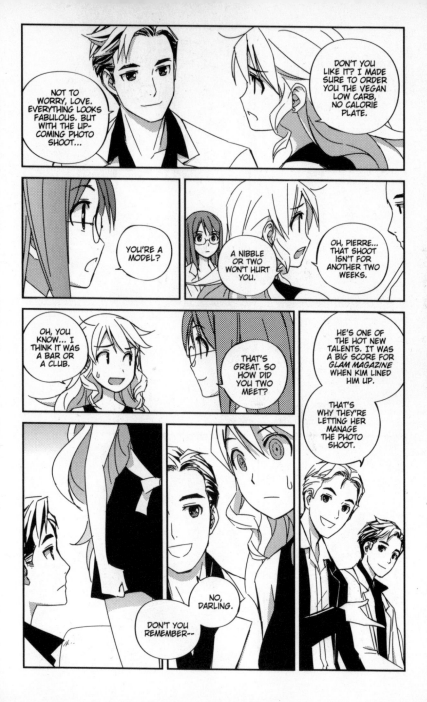

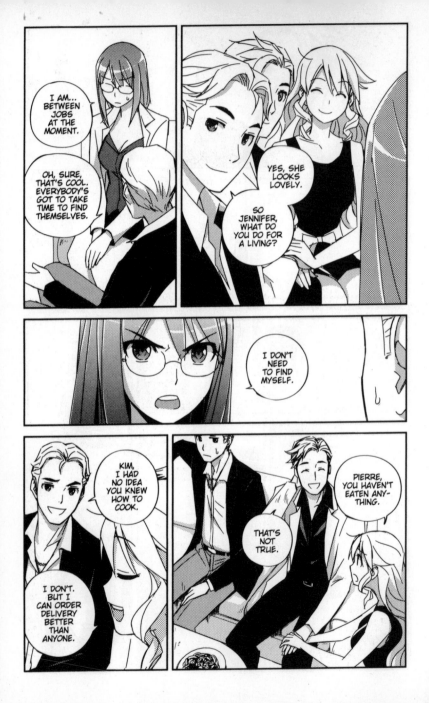

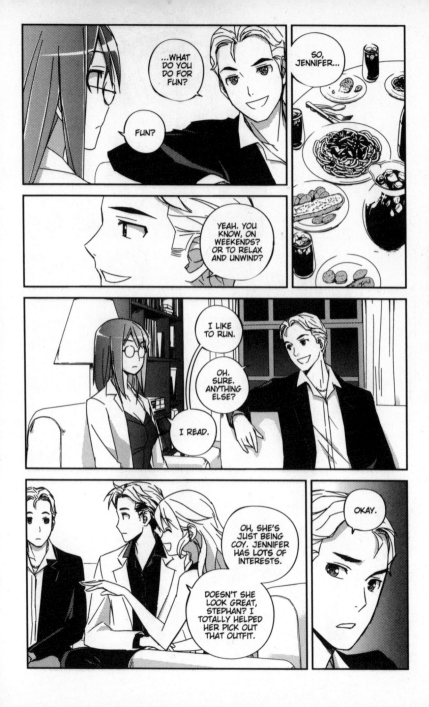

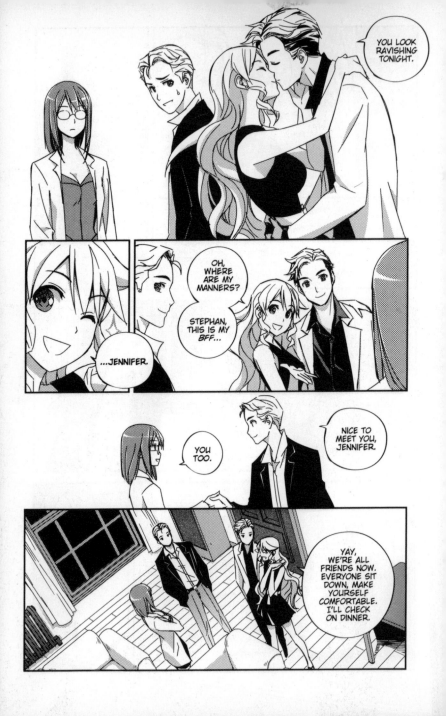

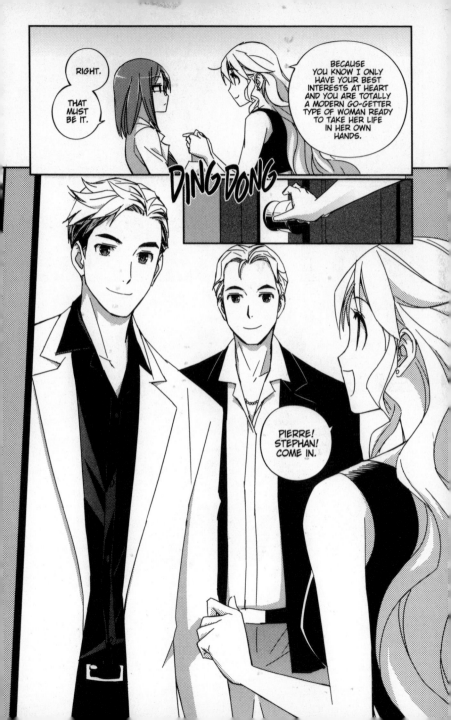

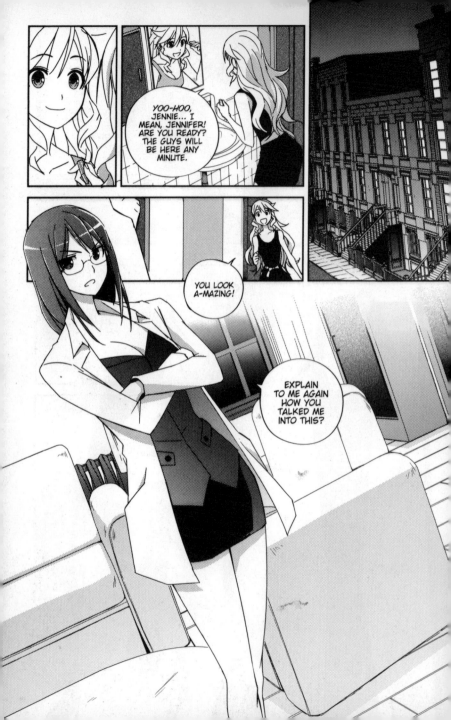

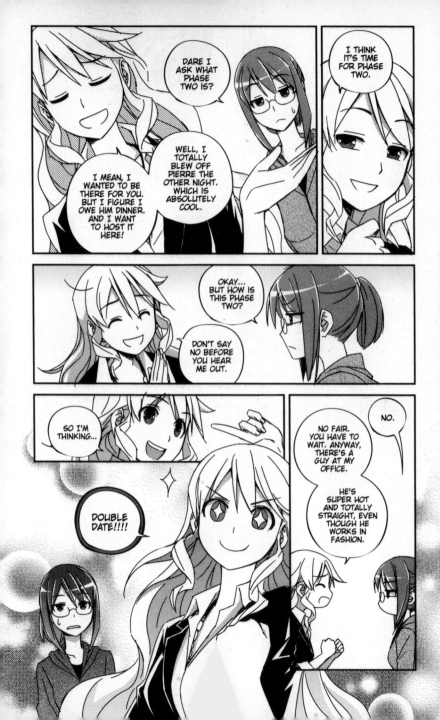

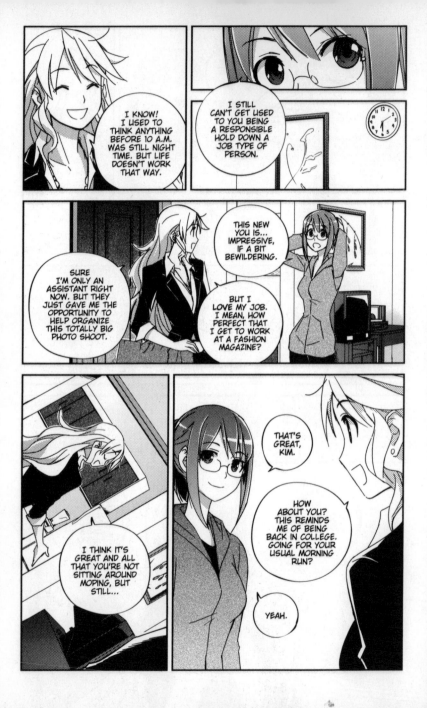

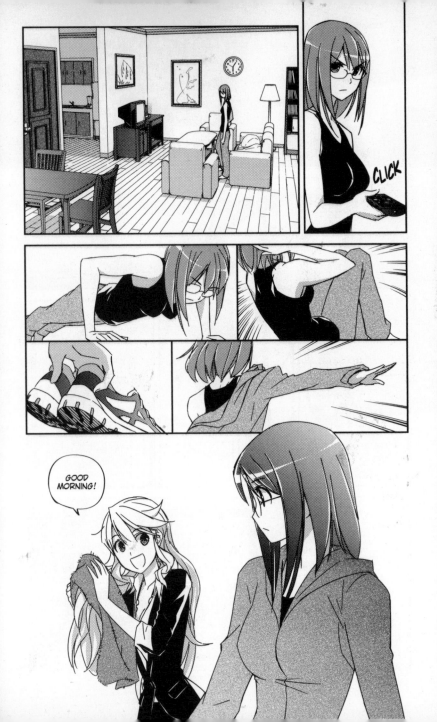

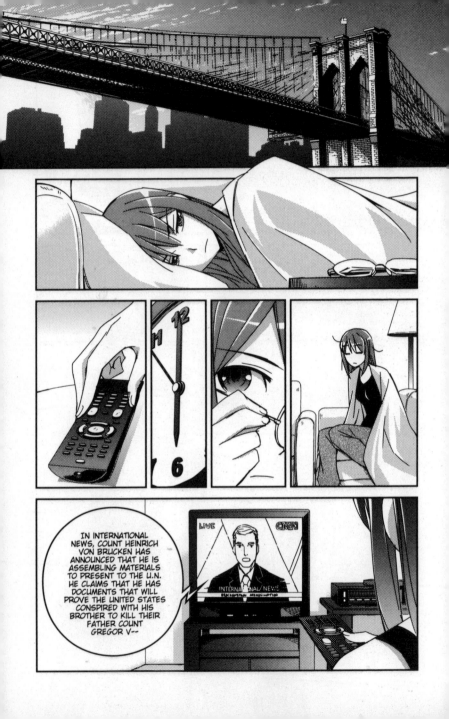

IN INTERNATIONAL NEWS, COUNT HEINRICH VON BRUCKEN HAS ANNOUNCED THAT HE IS ASSEMBLING MATERIALS TO PRESENT TO THE U.N. HE CLAIMS THAT HE HAS DOCUMENTS THAT WILL PROVE THE UNITED STATES CONSPIRED WITH HIS BROTHER TO KILL THEIR FATHER COUNT GREGOR V--

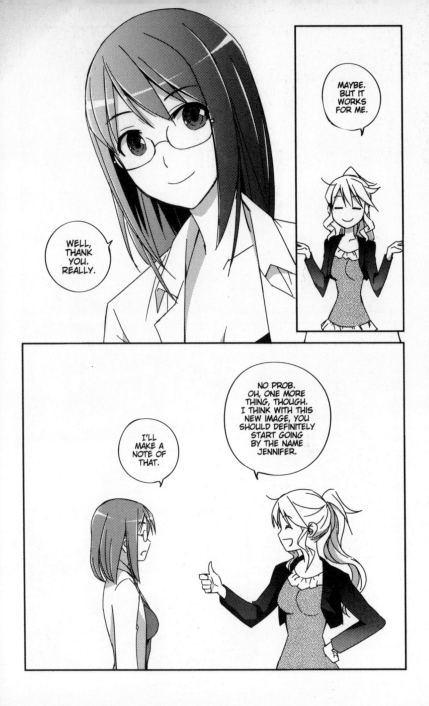

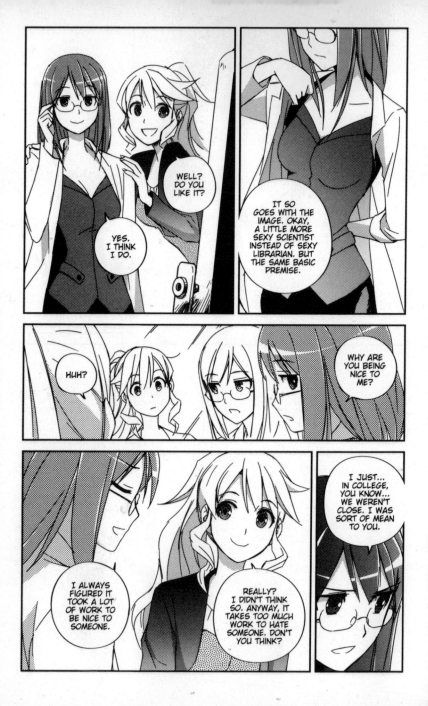

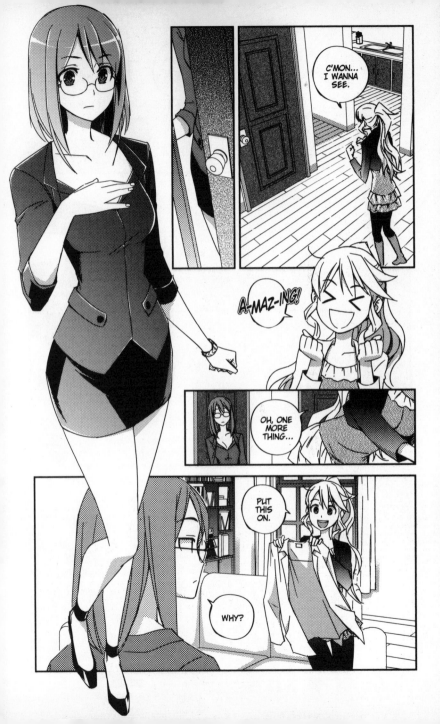

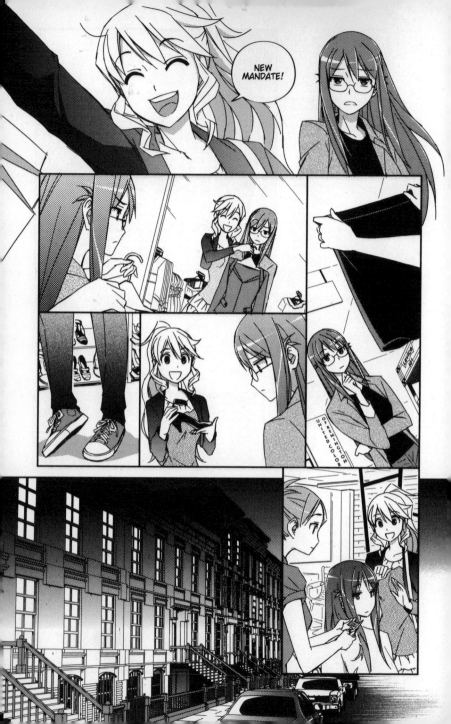

I DON'T KNOW, KIM... I REALLY DO APPRECIATE EVERYTHING YOU'VE DONE.
BUT I DON'T THINK IT'S WORKING.
YOU'RE RIGHT. THIS ISN'T THE RIGHT LOOK FOR YOU.
I KNOW. CONTACTS! WHAT IF WE TOOK OFF YOUR GLASSES...?
THERE.
BLINK BLINK
...
MMM... NO.
TURNS OUT YOU'RE ONE OF THOSE PEOPLE WHO LOOKS BETTER WITH GLASSES.

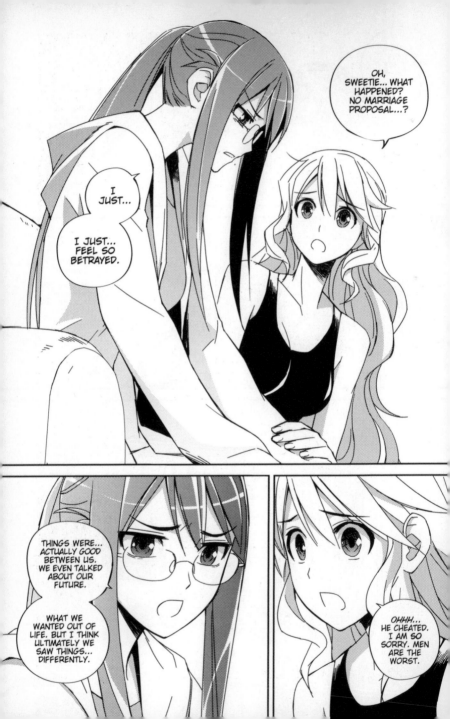

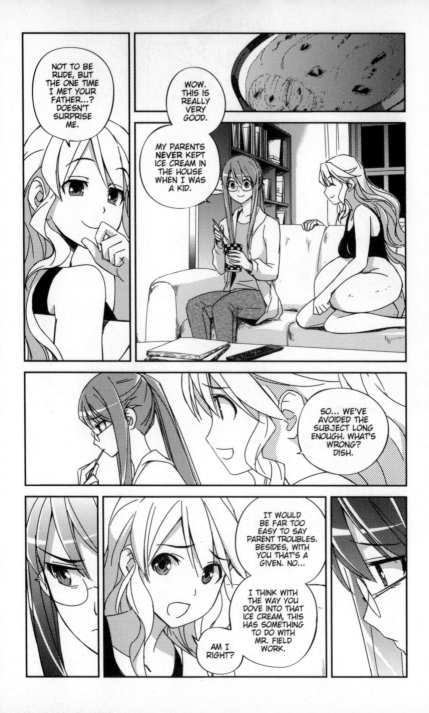

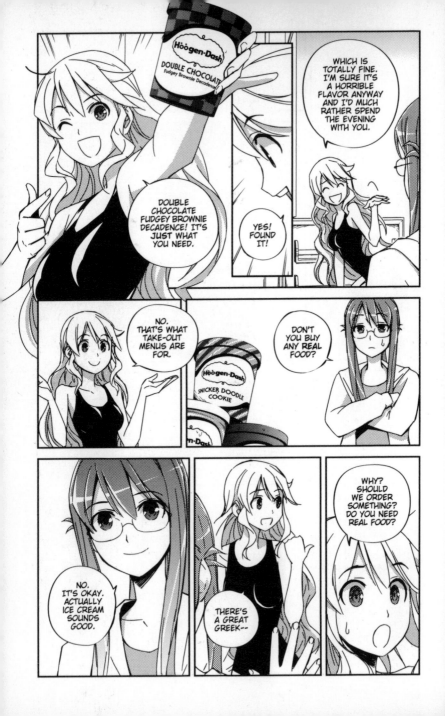

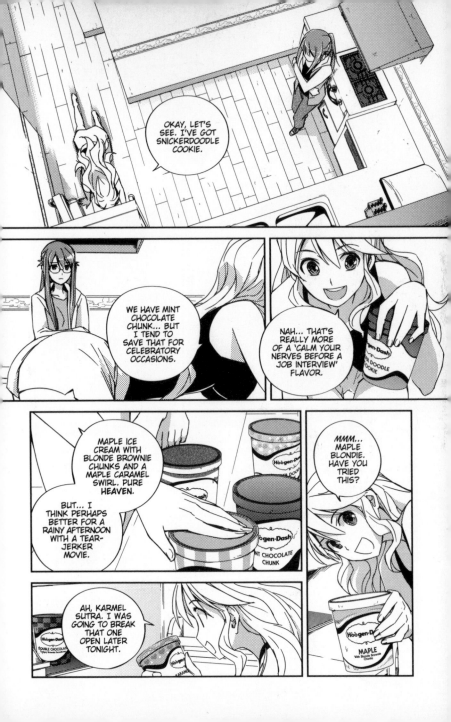

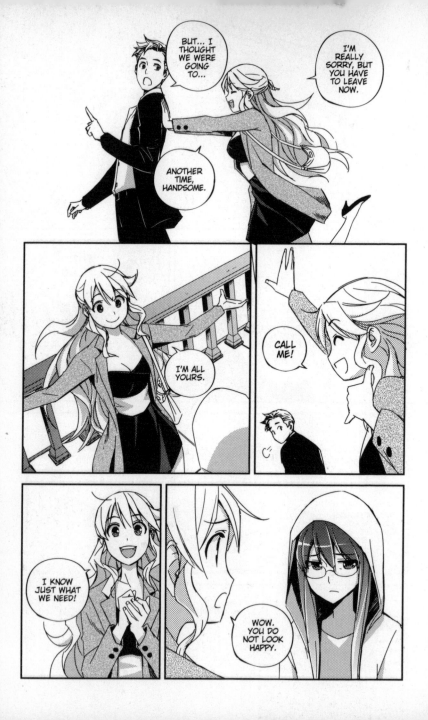

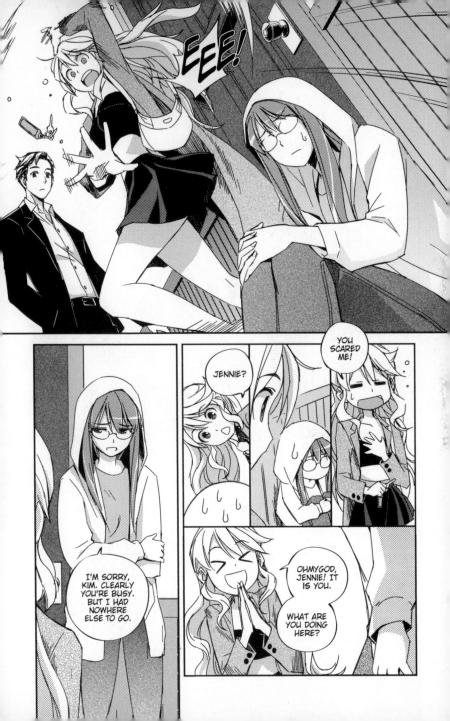

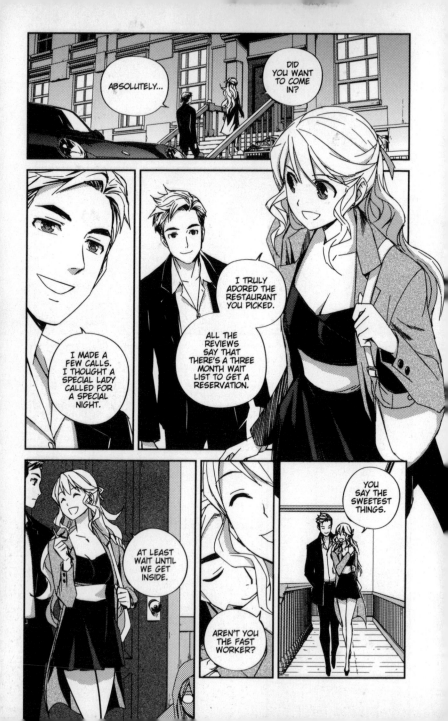

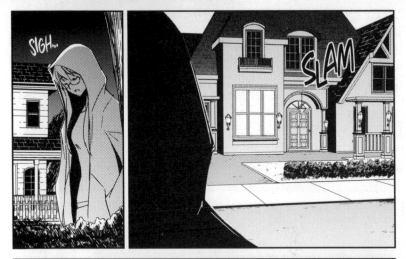

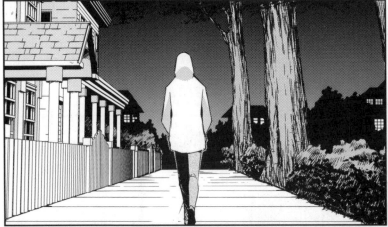

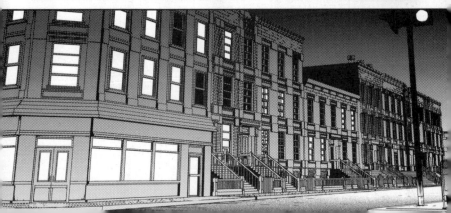

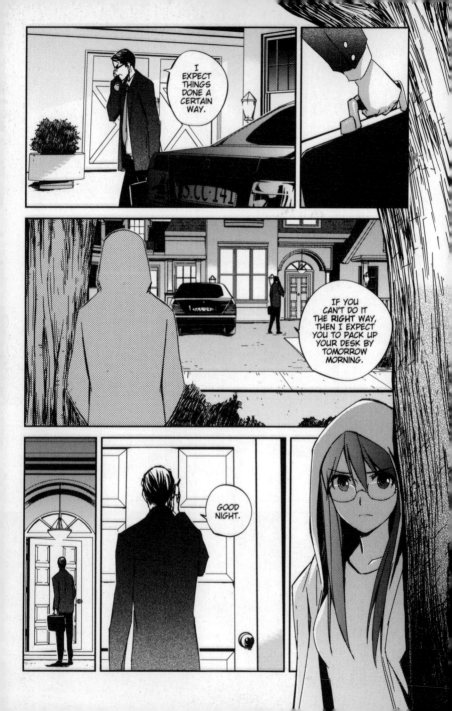

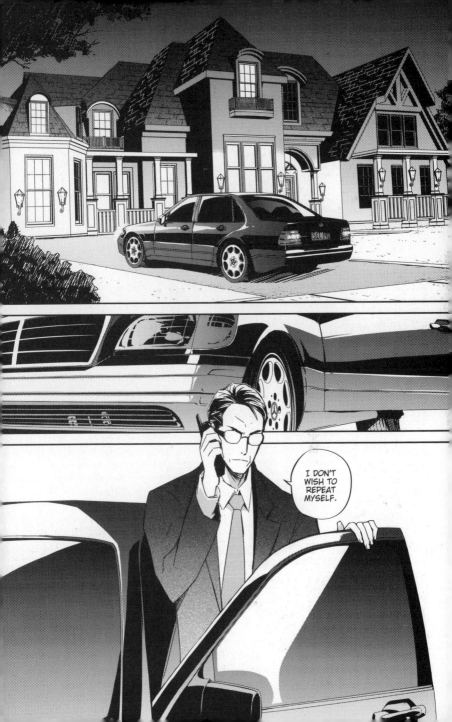

FILE 9:
INTERLUDE

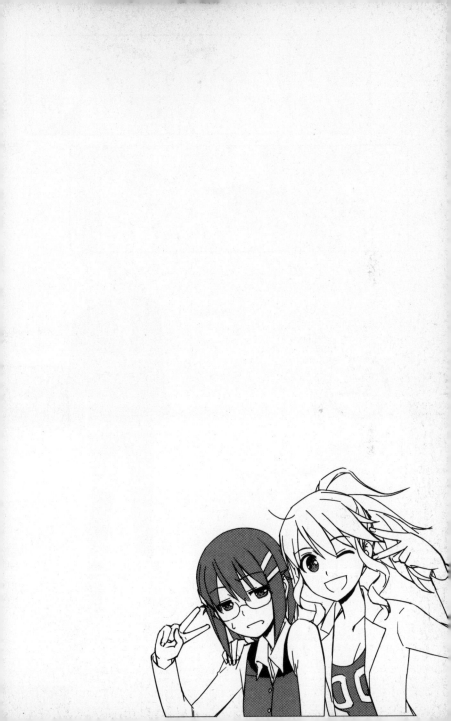

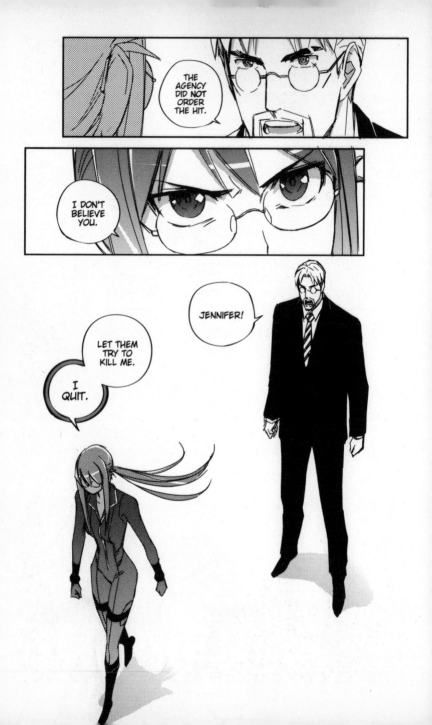

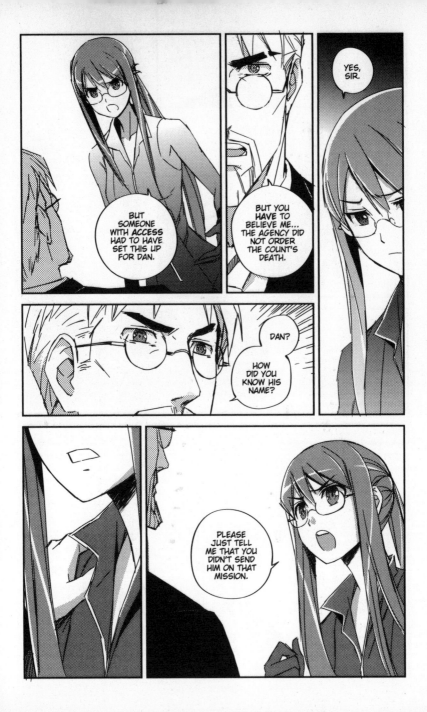

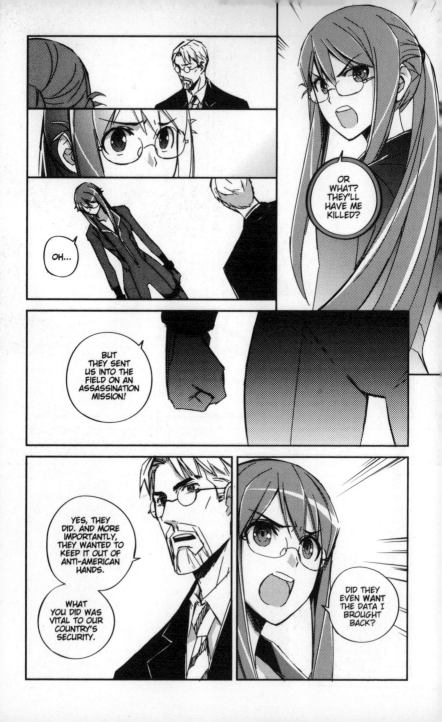

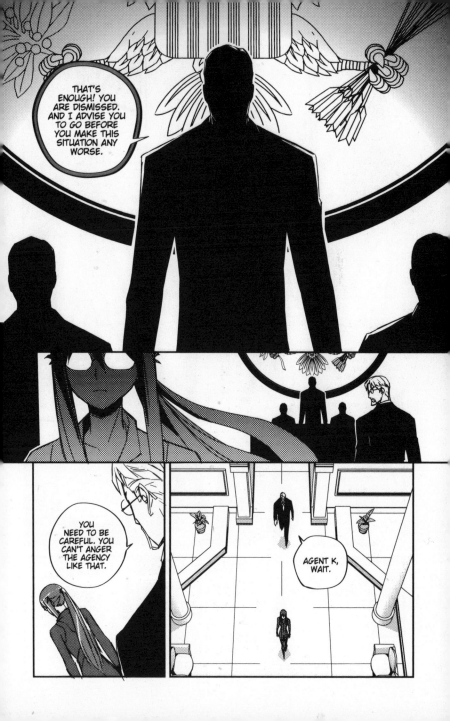

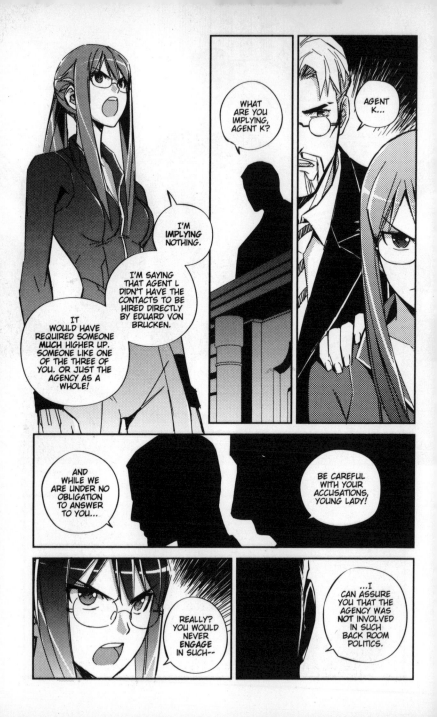

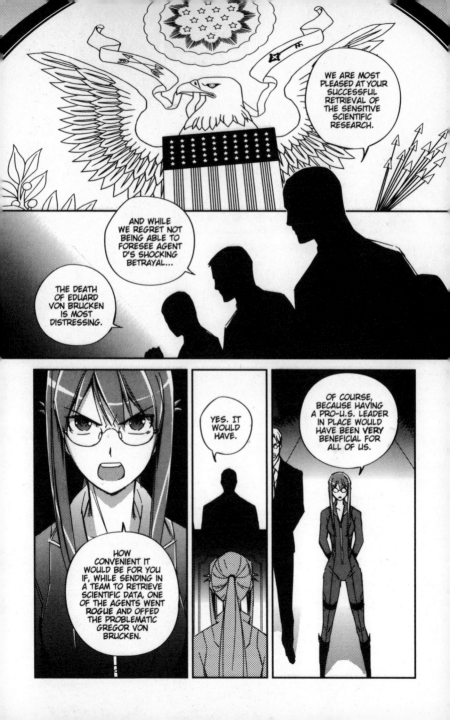

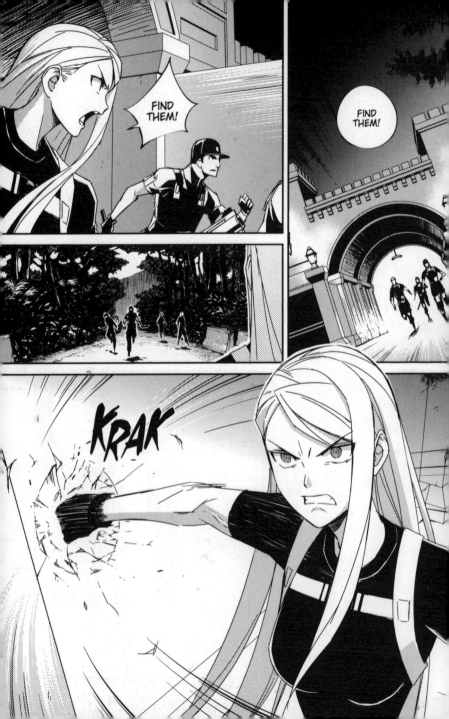

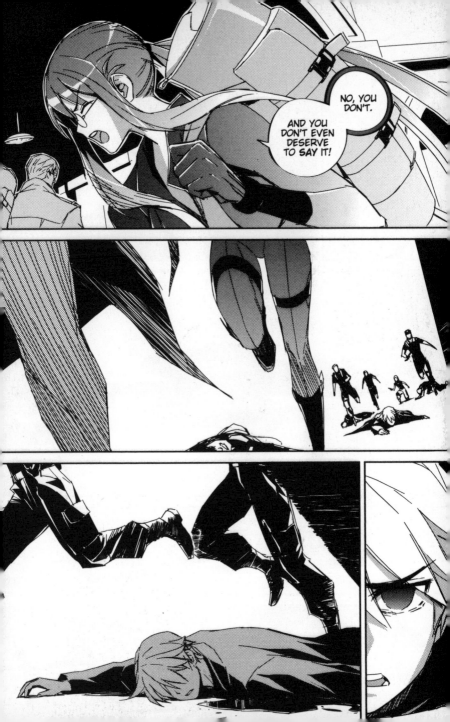

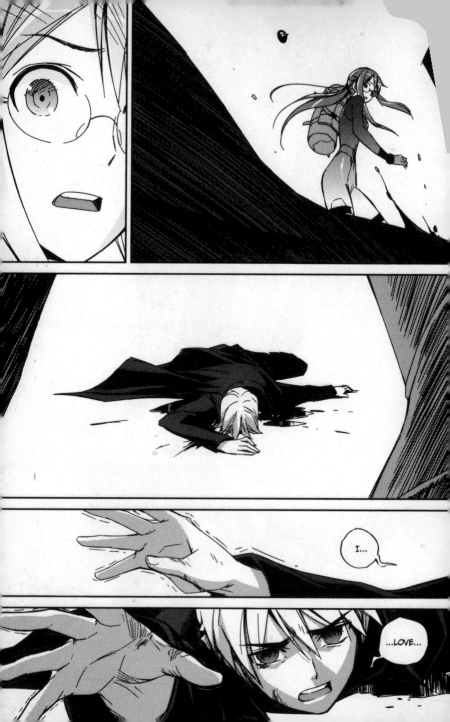

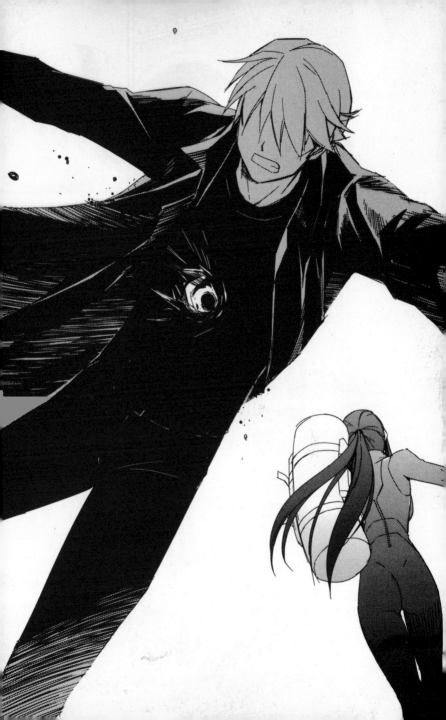

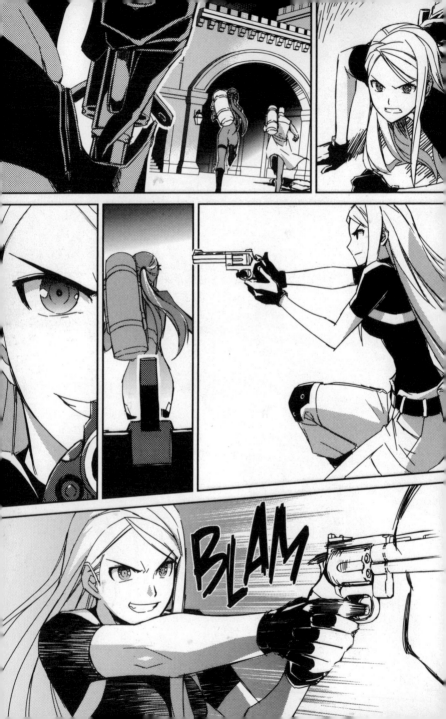

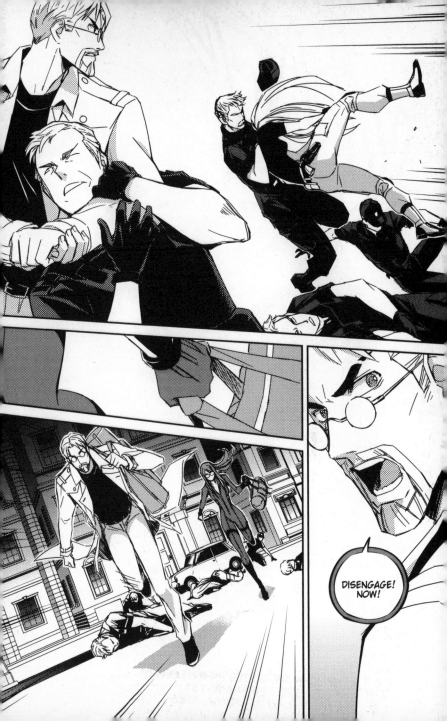

DISENGAGE! NOW!

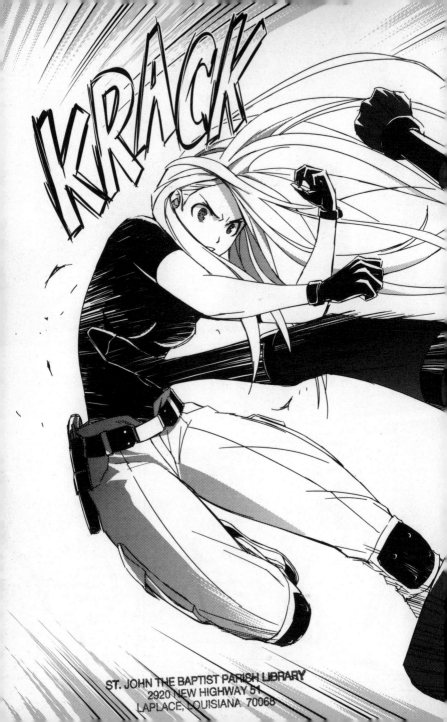

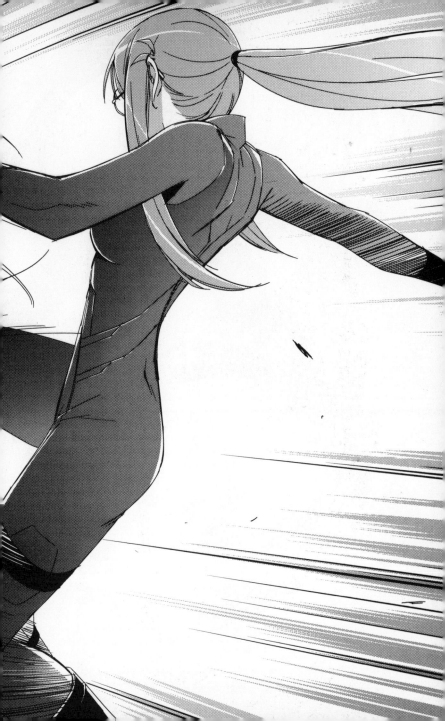

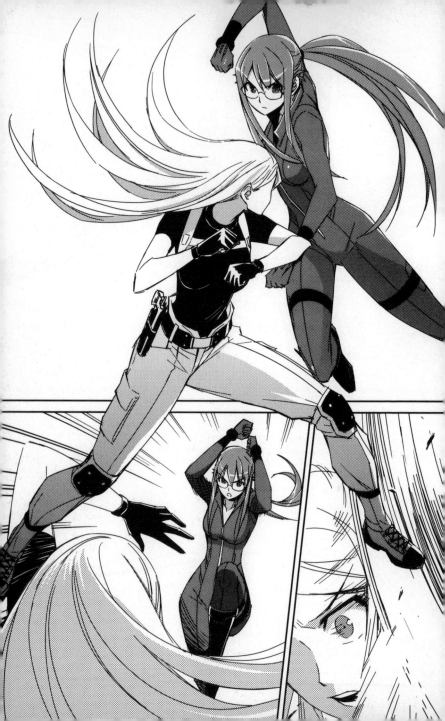

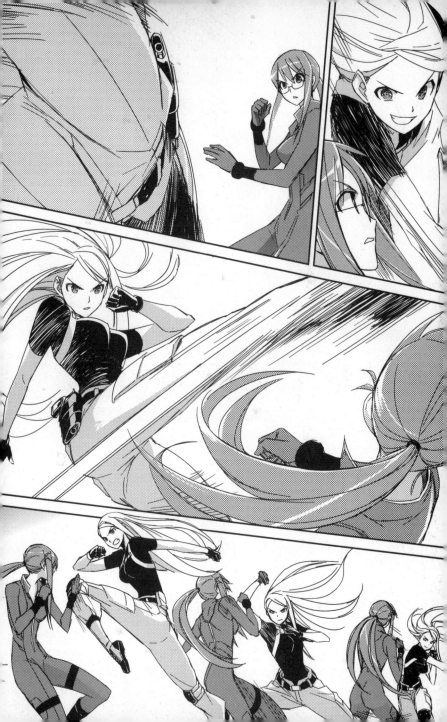

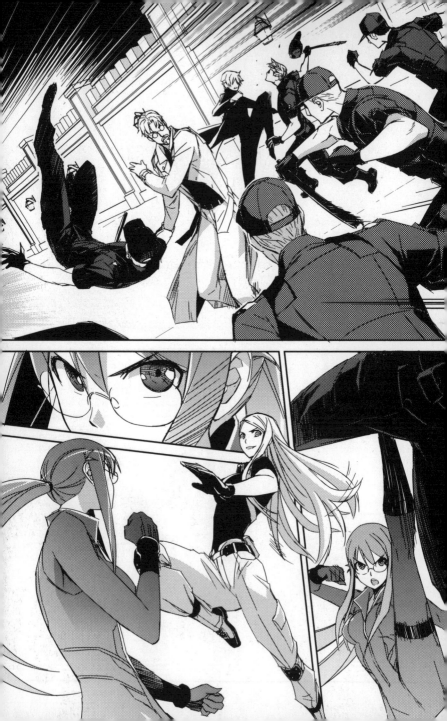

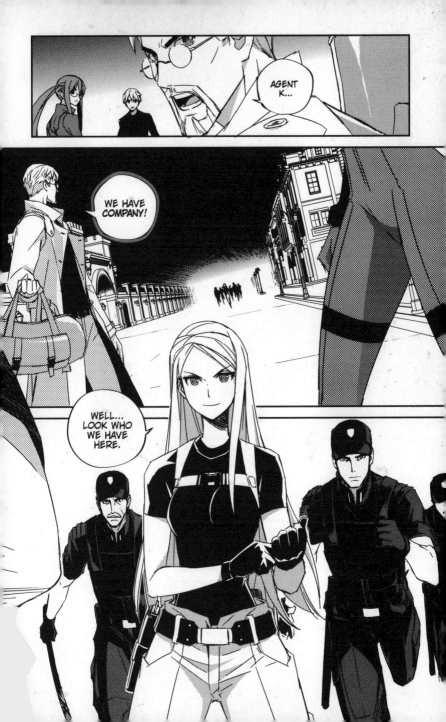

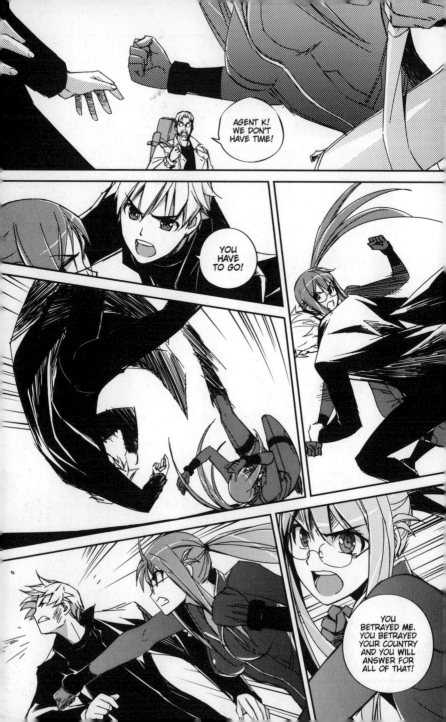

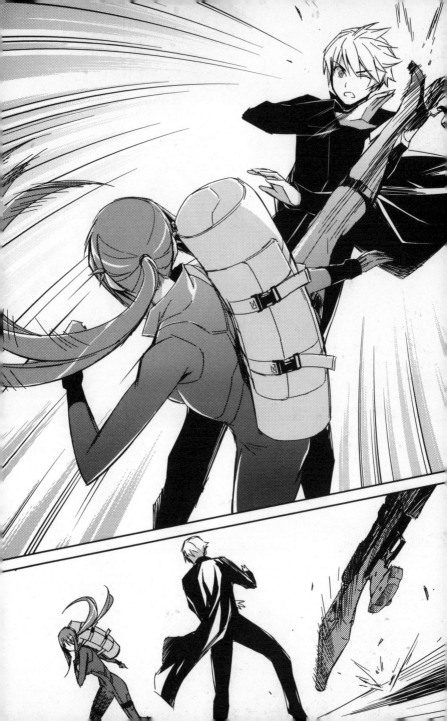

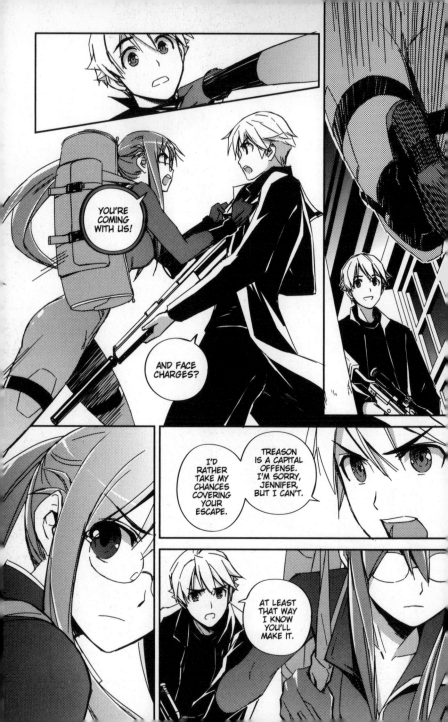

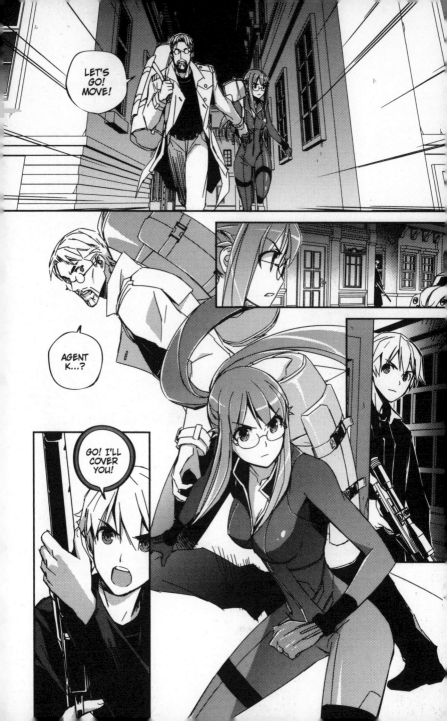

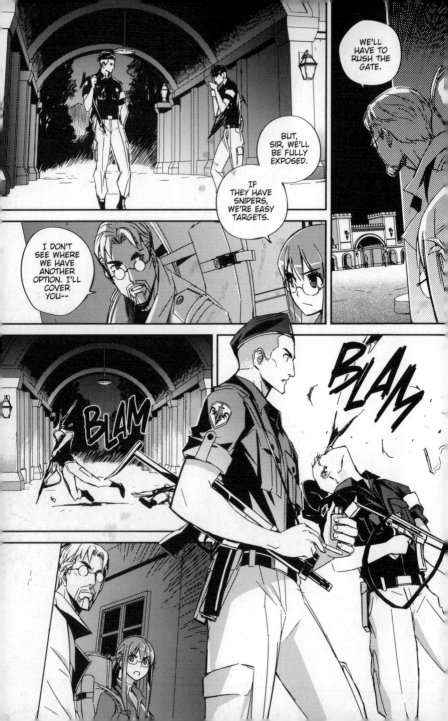

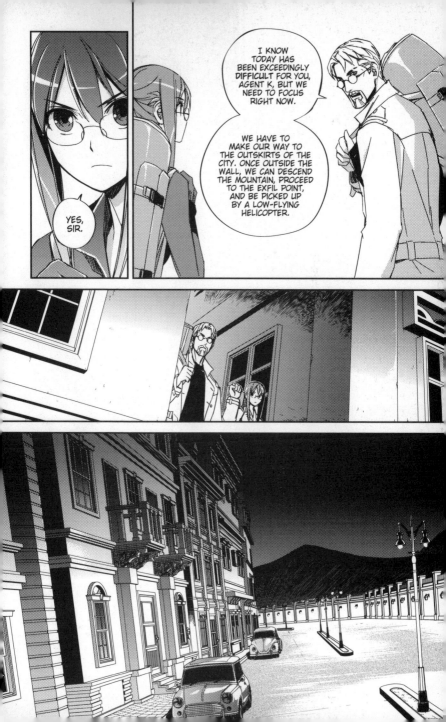

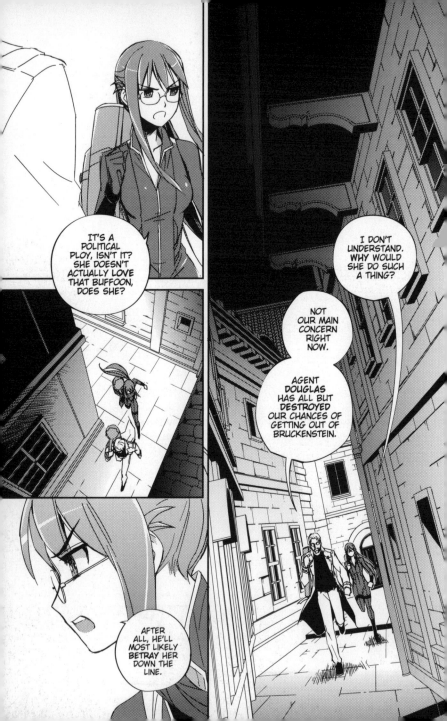

IT'S A POLITICAL PLOY, ISN'T IT? SHE DOESN'T ACTUALLY LOVE THAT BUFFOON, DOES SHE?

I DON'T UNDERSTAND. WHY WOULD SHE DO SUCH A THING?

NOT OUR MAIN CONCERN RIGHT NOW.

AGENT DOUGLAS HAS ALL BUT DESTROYED OUR CHANCES OF GETTING OUT OF BRUCKENSTEIN.

AFTER ALL, HE'LL MOST LIKELY BETRAY HER DOWN THE LINE.

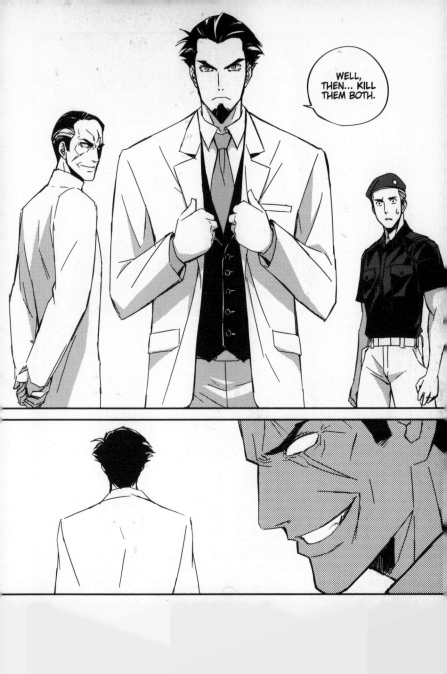

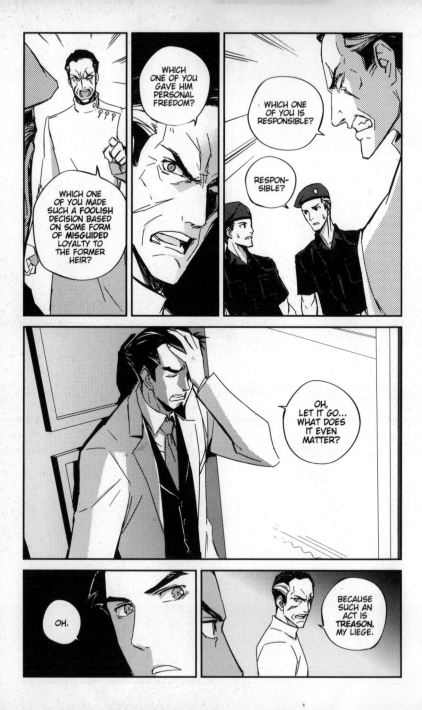

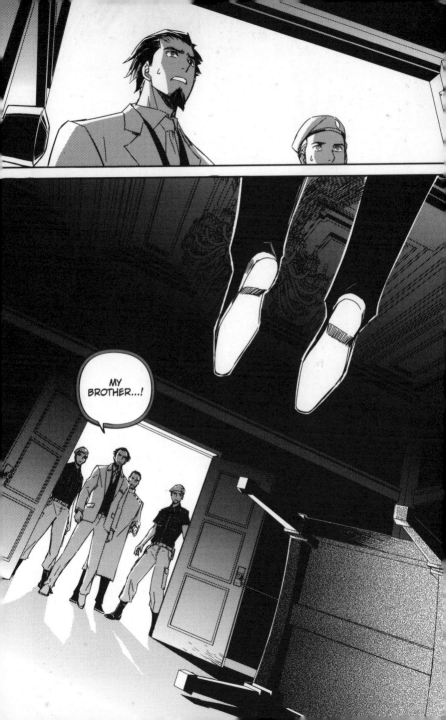

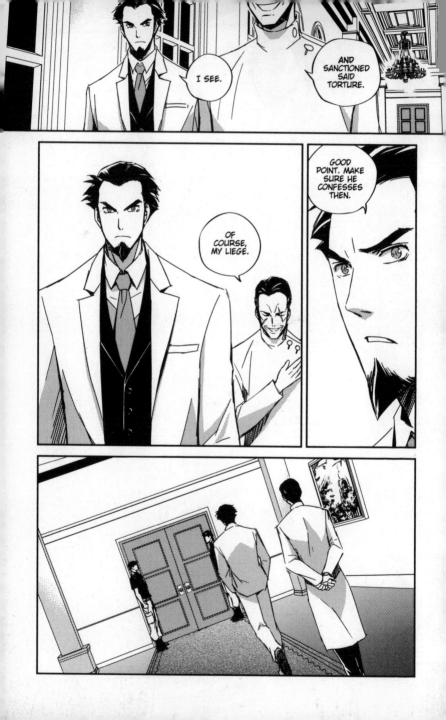

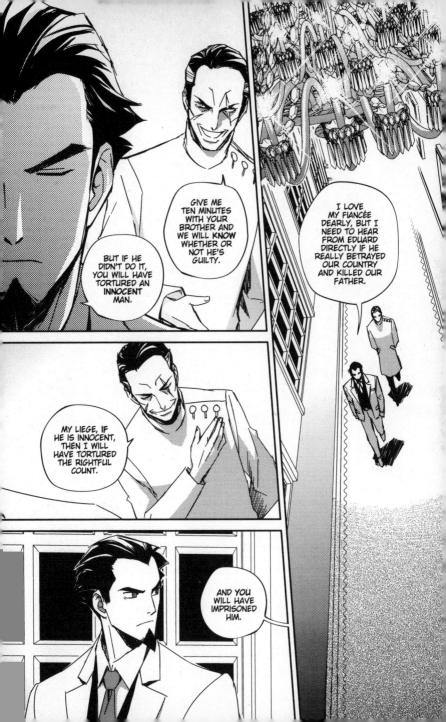

FILE 8:
UNHAPPY ENDINGS

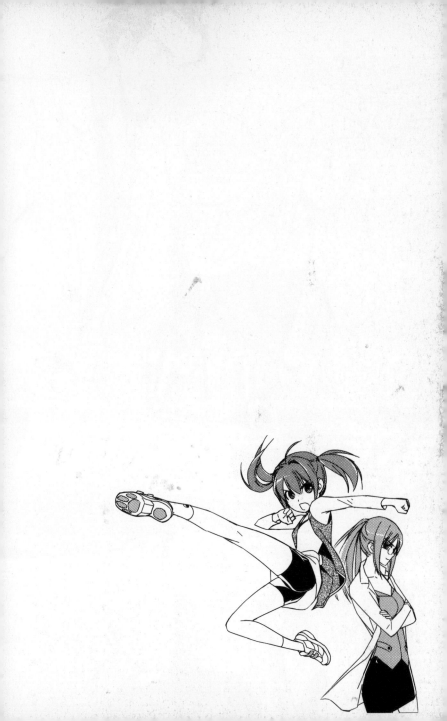

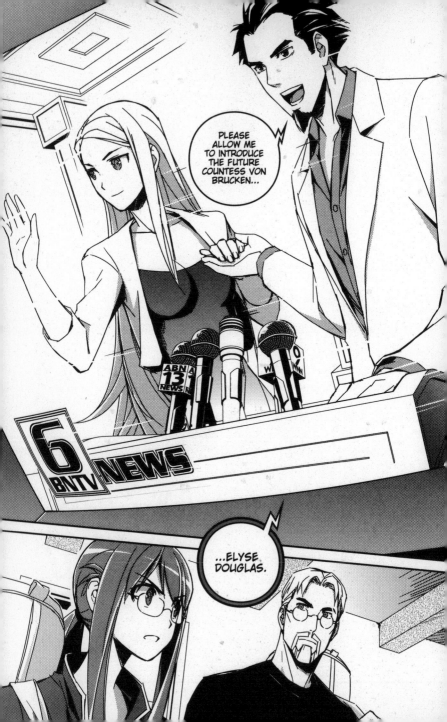

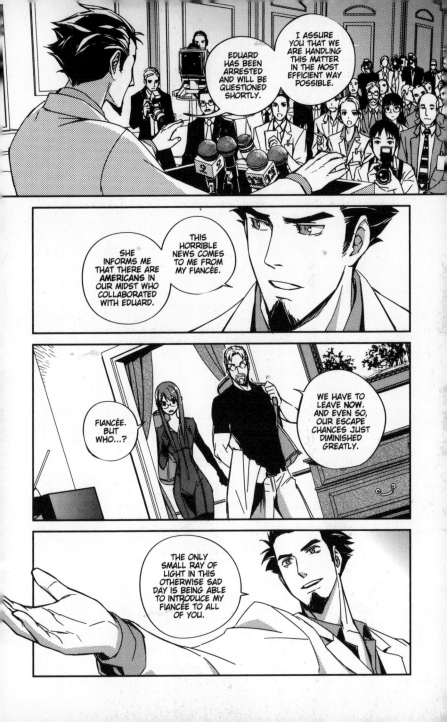

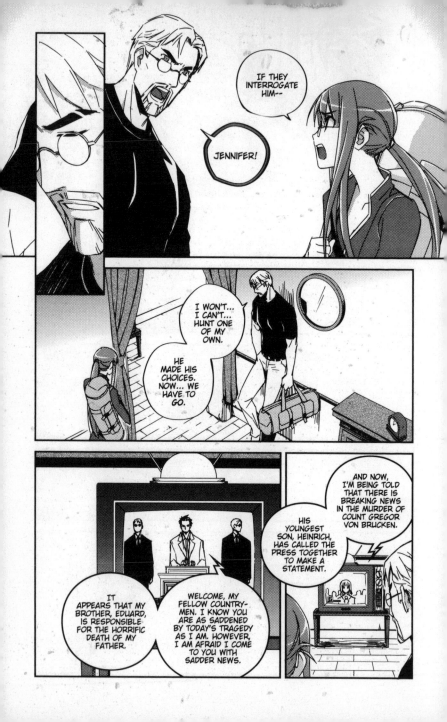

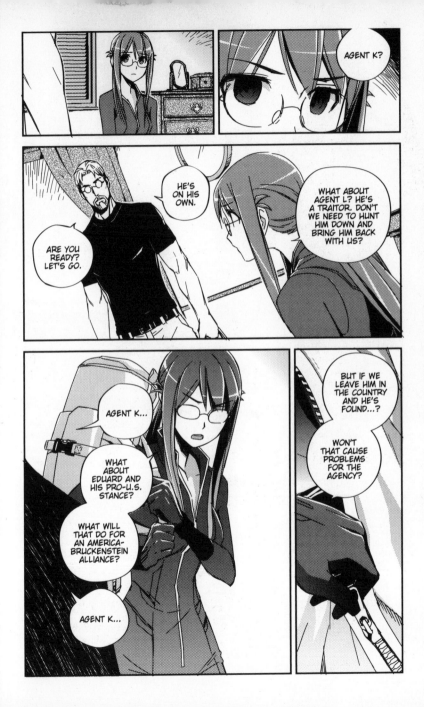

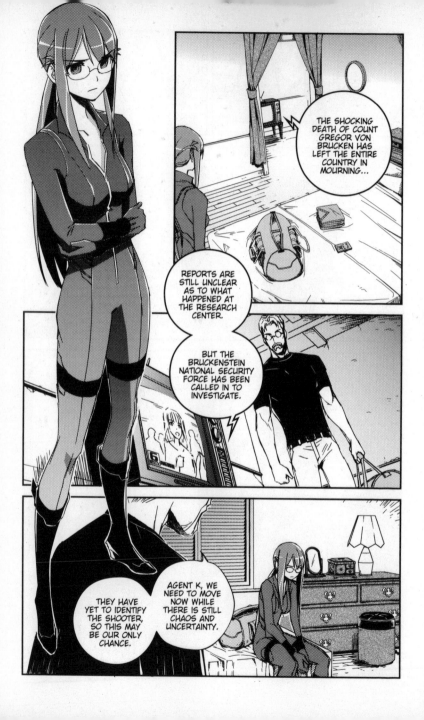

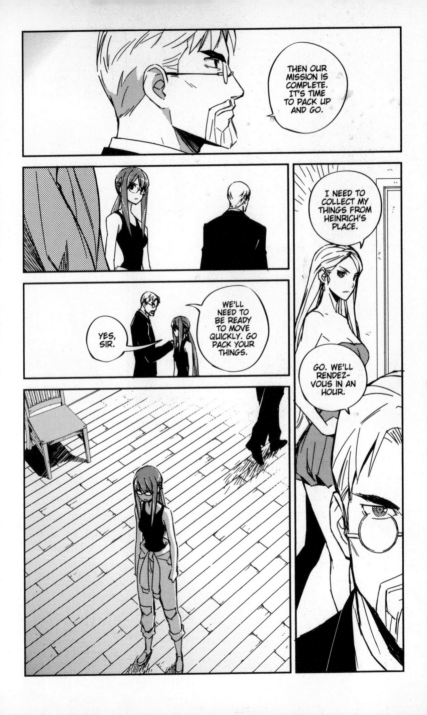

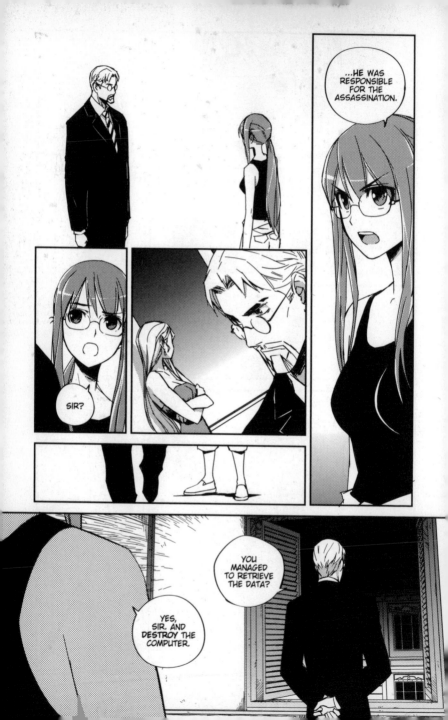

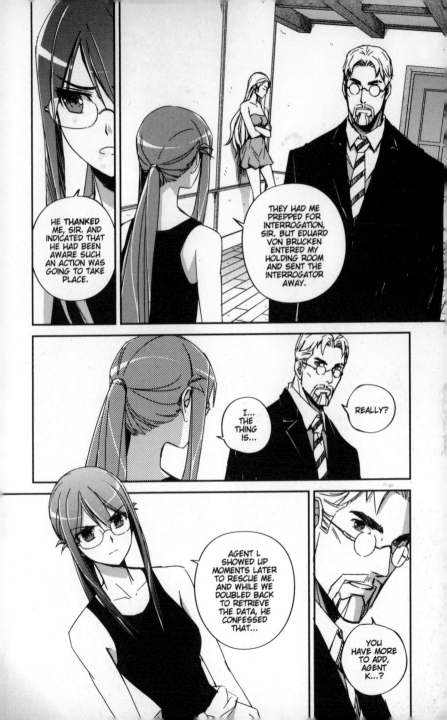

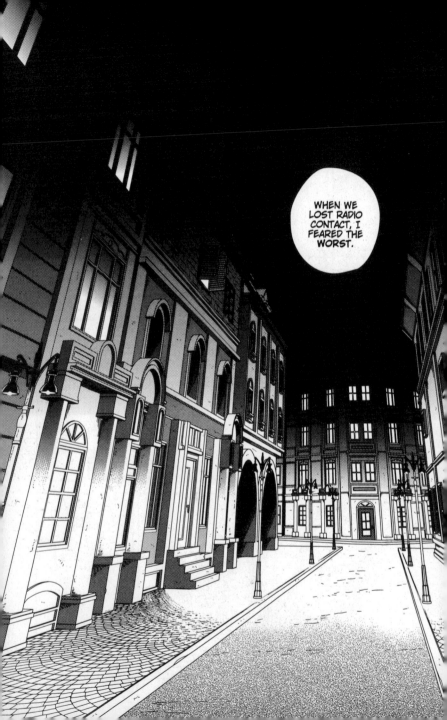

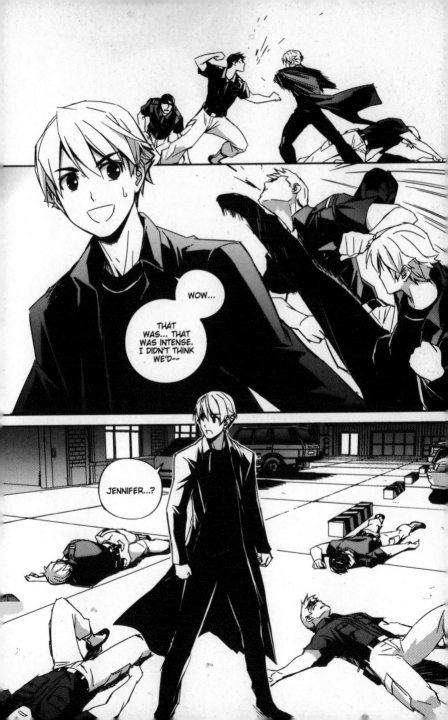

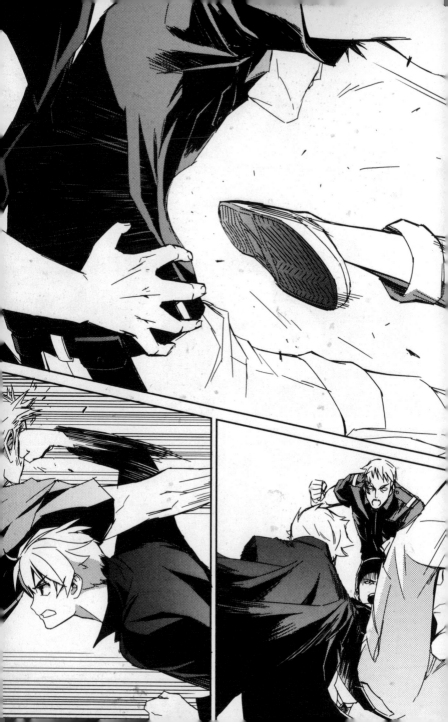

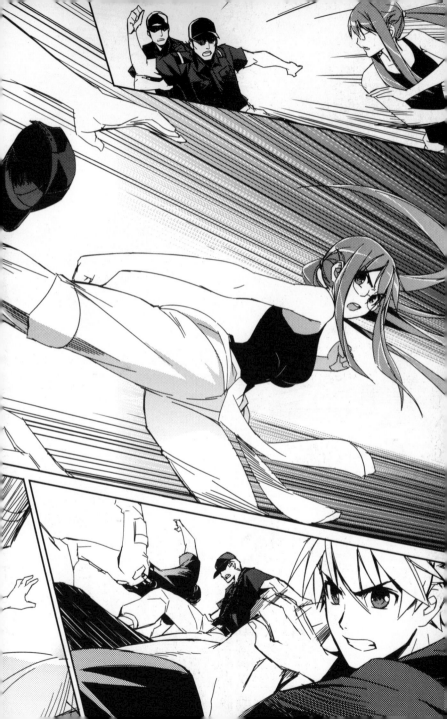

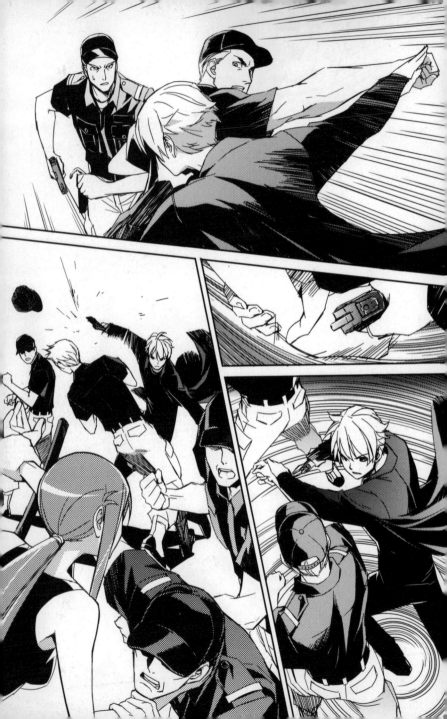

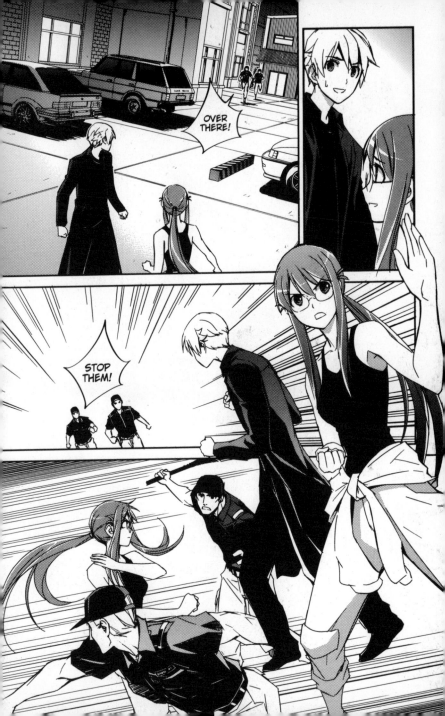

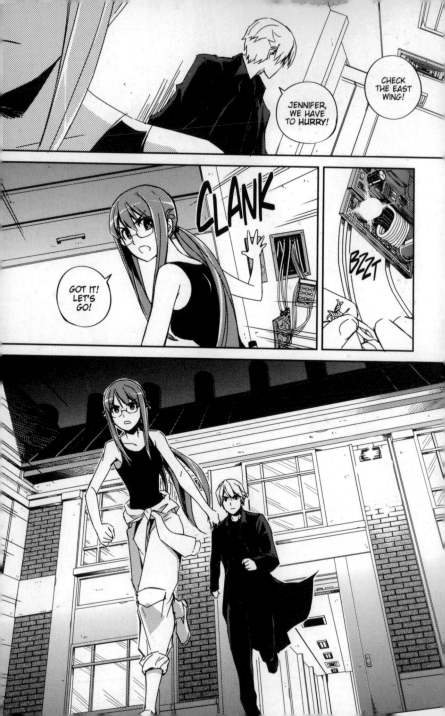

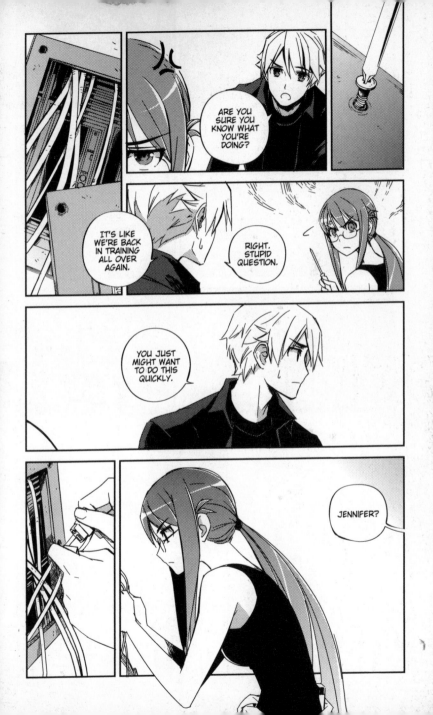

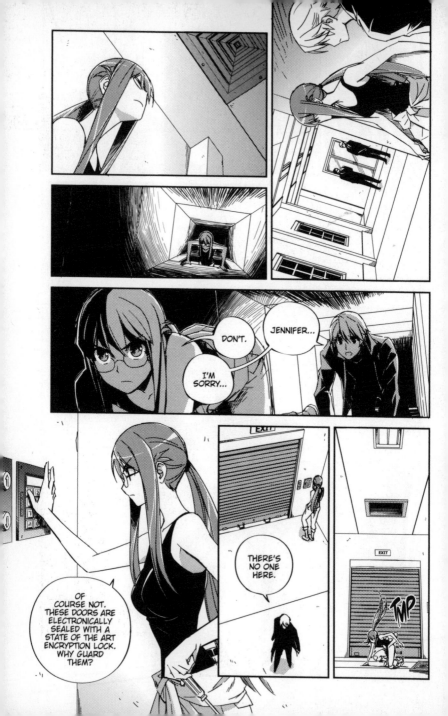

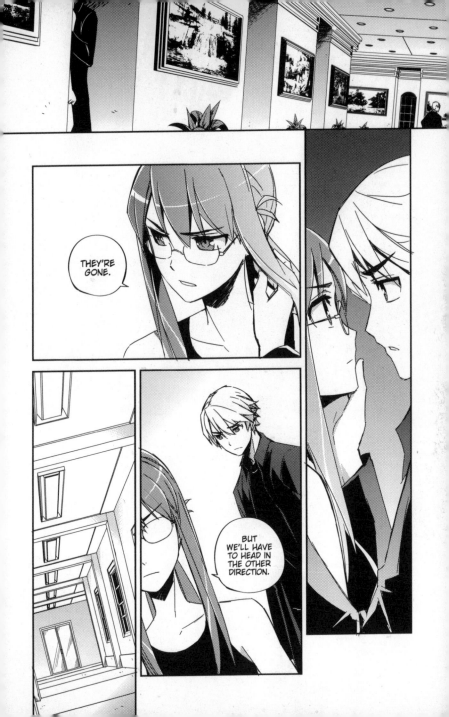

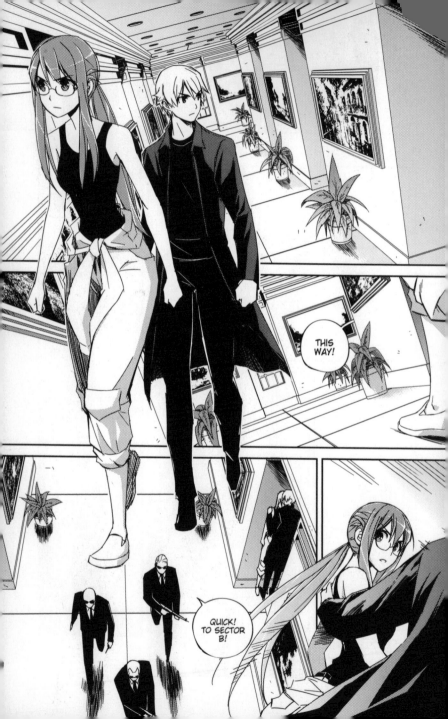

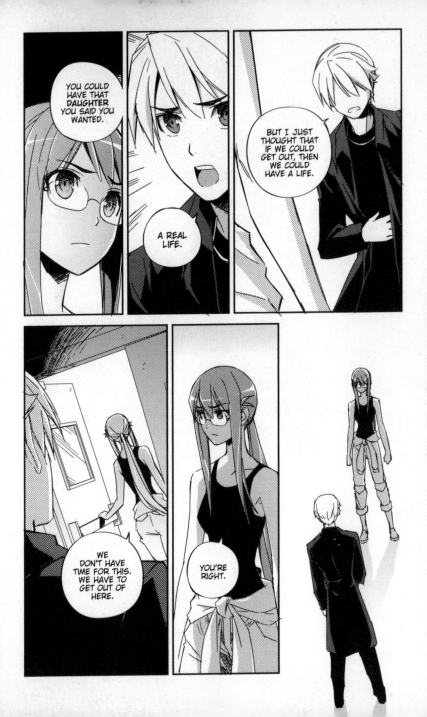

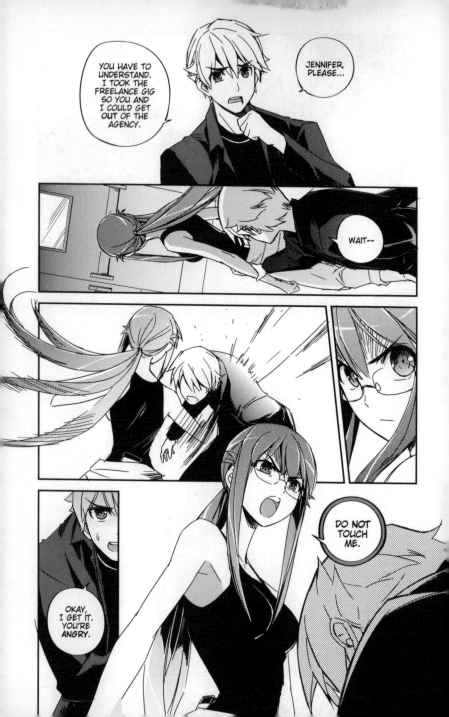

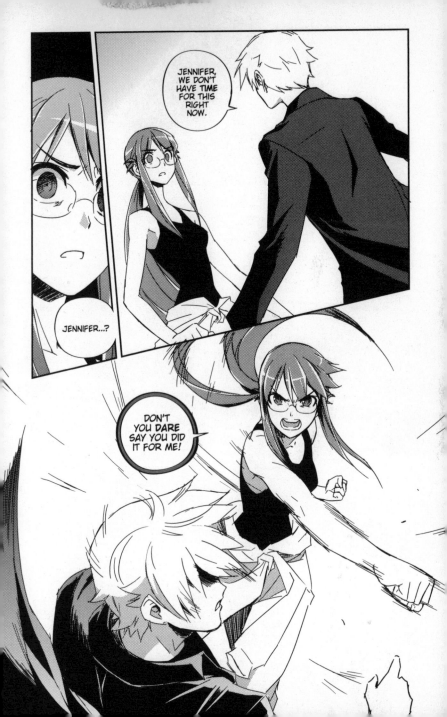

```
FILE 7:
SO MISLED
```

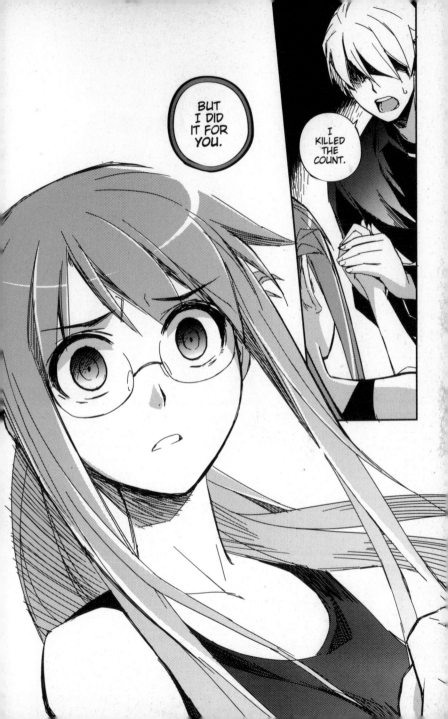

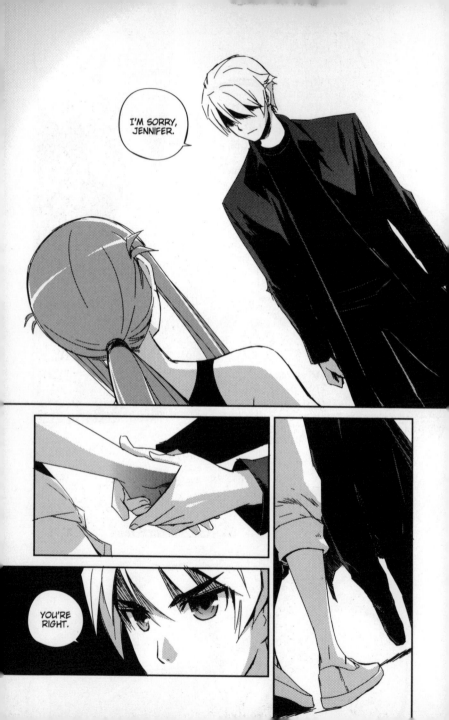

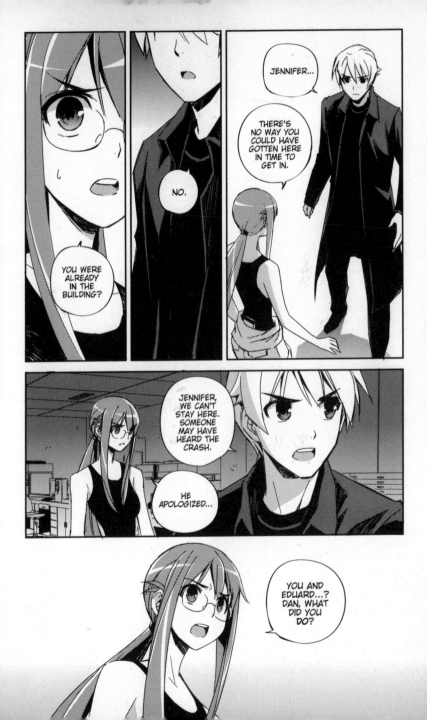

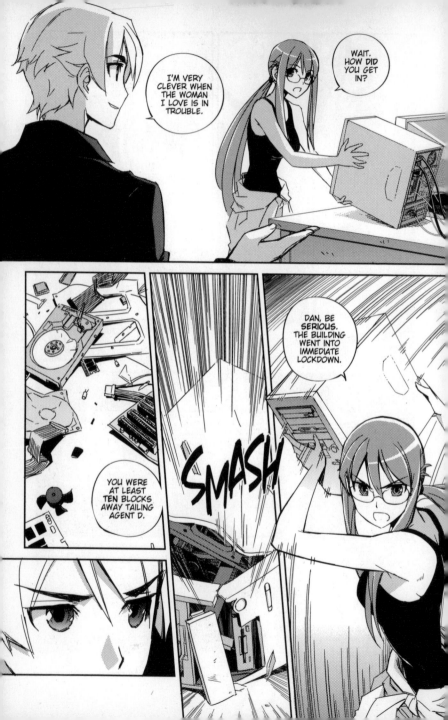

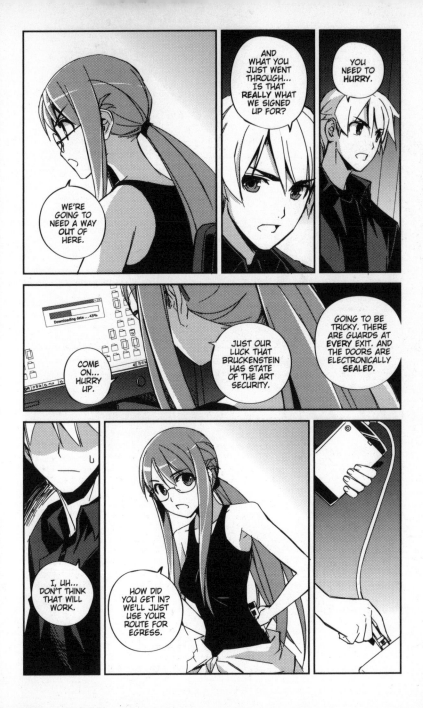

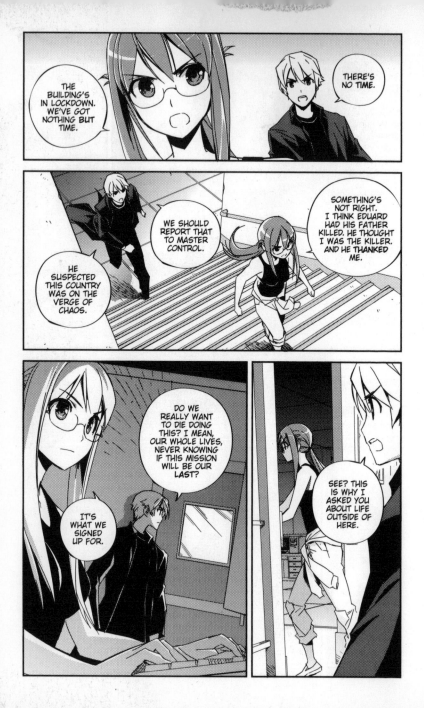

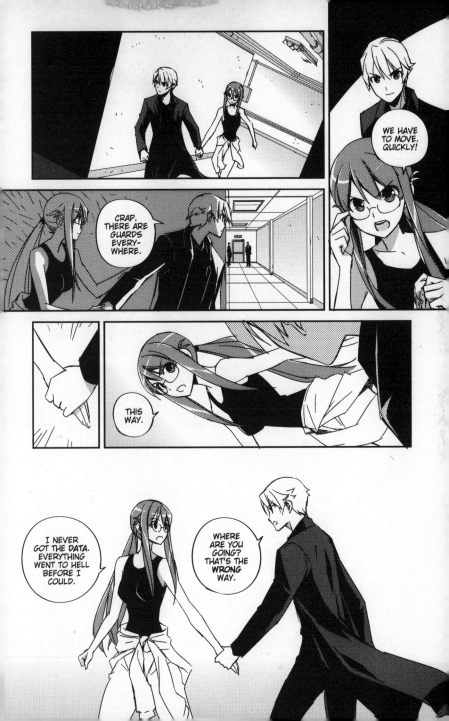

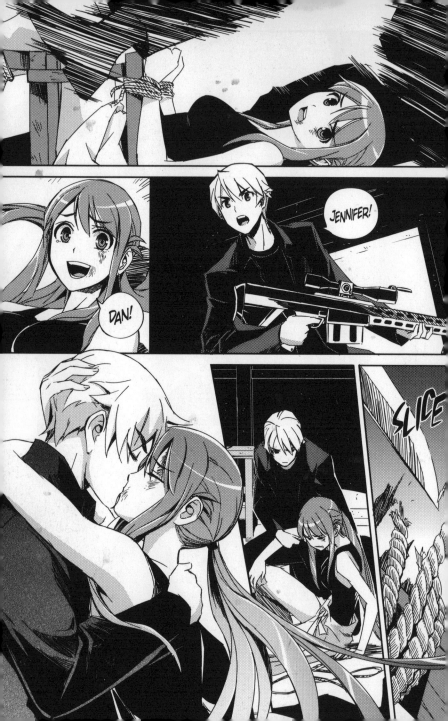

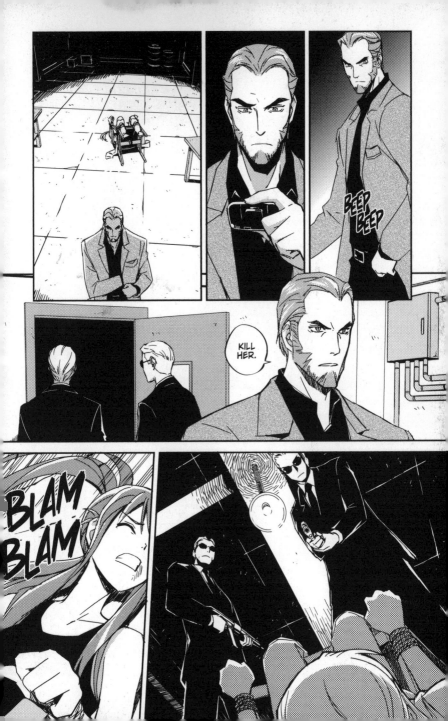

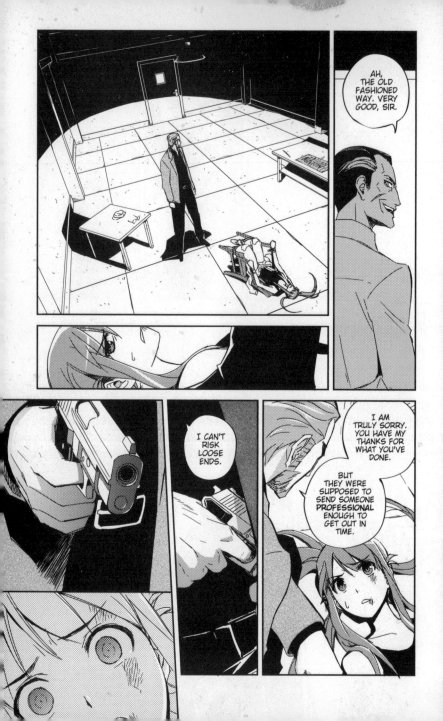

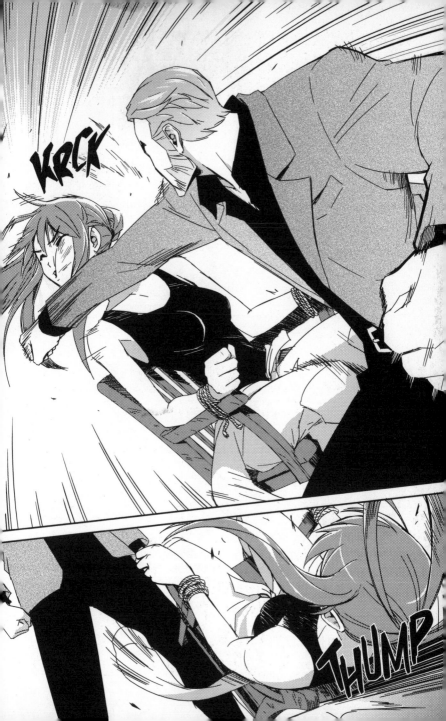

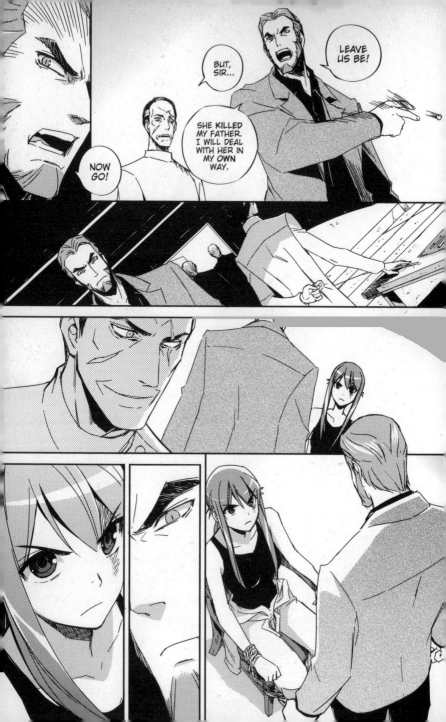

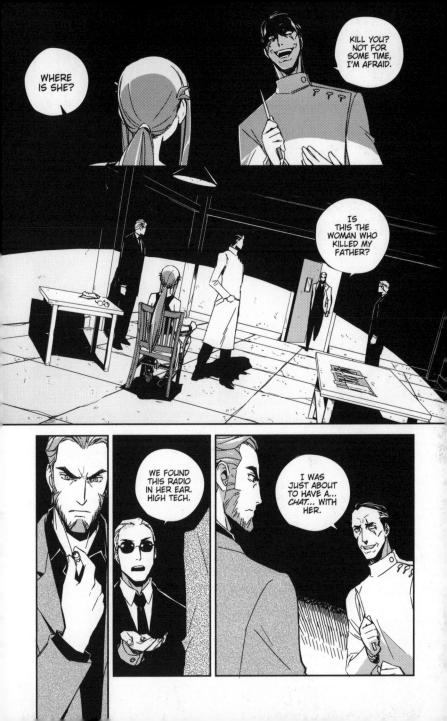

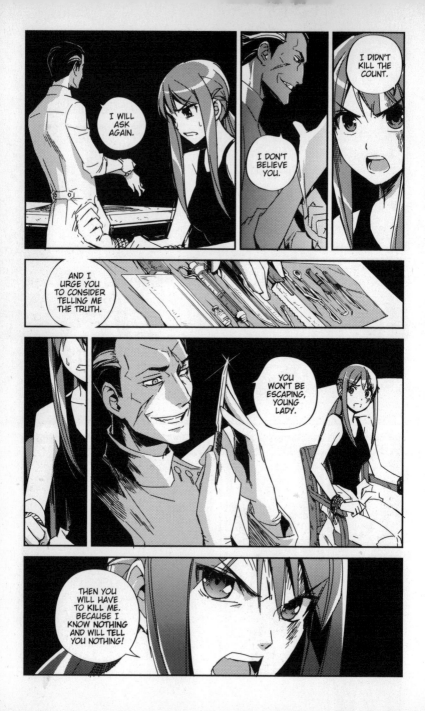

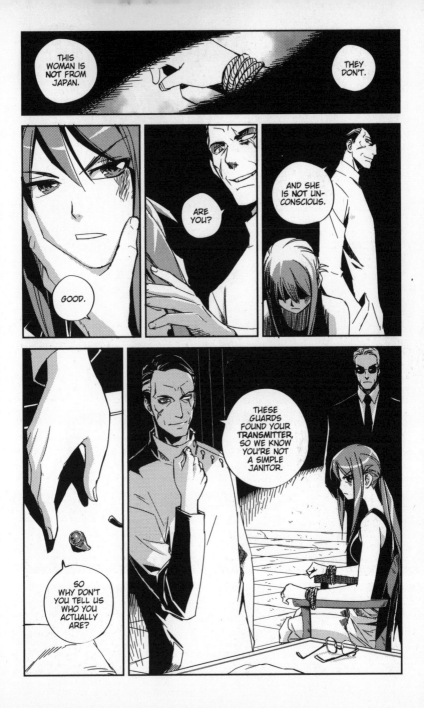

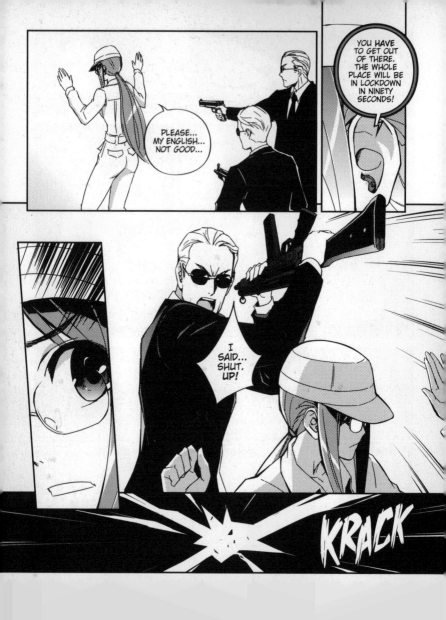

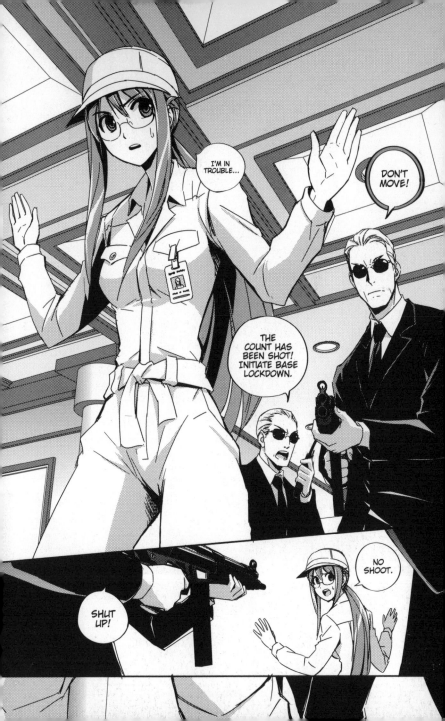

FILE 6:
CAPTURED

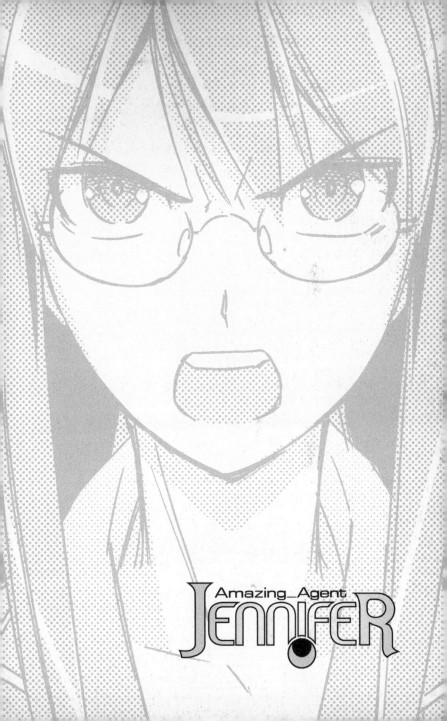

AGENT ASSESSMENT FORM

REPORT PRODUCED AT	DATE PRODUCED	FILE PROCESS

PERSONAL NOTES

* I believe this mission has placed Agent K in great danger. Bruckenstein seems to be on the verge of a civil war. Gregor Von Brucken **(see attached file and photo)**, the current Count, has relations with the United States, and the theft of this research may have ended them entirely. While his heir, Eduard Von Brucken **(see attached file and photo)** remains a U.S. ally, he is bound to his father's will. The Count's second son, Heinrich, is the wild card in this scenario. He is currently a playboy and has little ambition but is recklessly amoral.

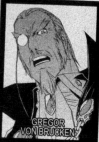

GREGOR VON BRUCKEN

* I have become aware that Agent K is involved romantically with Agent L, who even attended her graduation from college. In fact, he was the only person there to congratulate her, save for her freshman-year roommate, Kim Donovan **(see attached file and photo)**, who is someone to whom Agent K is not at all close. Her isolation may have drawn her to Agent L. This concerns me, as for Agent L to attend the event means that the two agents have shared their real names. This is against regulations. To protect her career, I have struck all mentions of this affair and the graduation from Agency records.

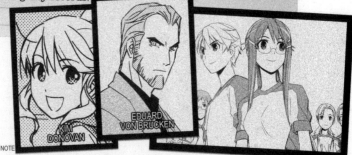

KIM DONOVAN

EDUARD VON BRUCKEN

FIELD NOTE

The mission has gone south. Agent K was in the lab when an assassin's bullets struck Count Gregor. The facility is about to go into lockdown and with Agent L tasked with providing backup for Agent D, this leaves Agent K trapped inside alone!

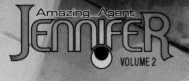

Amazing Agent
JENNIFER
VOLUME 2

art by **Kriss Sison**
story by **Nunzio DeFilippis & Christina Weir**

STAFF CREDITS

lettering	**Nicky Lim**
art assists	**Rafael Cal-Ortiz, Jaimee Delos Santos, Ian Olympia, Paolo Antonio Aguasin, Mark Henry Bustamante**
layout	**Adam Arnold**
design	**Nicky Lim**
copy editor	**Shanti Whitesides**
editor	**Adam Arnold**
publisher	**Jason DeAngelis Seven Seas Entertainment**

AMAZING AGENT JENNIFER VOL. 2
Copyright © 2012 Seven Seas Entertainment, LLC and Nunzio DeFilippis and Christina Weir.

ISBN: 978-1-935934-09-7

Printed in the USA

First Printing: January 2012

10 9 8 7 6 5 4 3 2 1

FOLLOW US ONLINE: **www.gomanga.com**

READING DIRECTIONS

This book reads from *right to left*, Japanese style. If this is your first time reading manga, you start reading from the top right panel on each page and take it from there. If you get lost, just follow the numbered diagram here. It may seem backwards at first, but you'll get the hang of it! Have fun!!

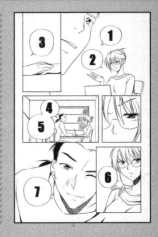

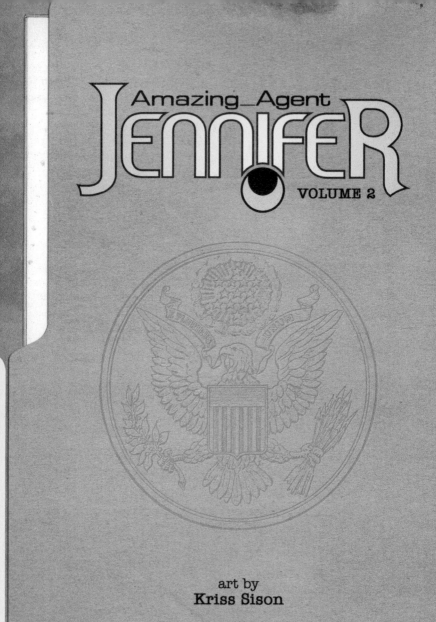

Amazing Agent
JENNIFER
VOLUME 2

art by
Kriss Sison

story by
Nunzio DeFilippis
and **Christina Weir**